LESSON FOR A HAPPY MARRIAGE™

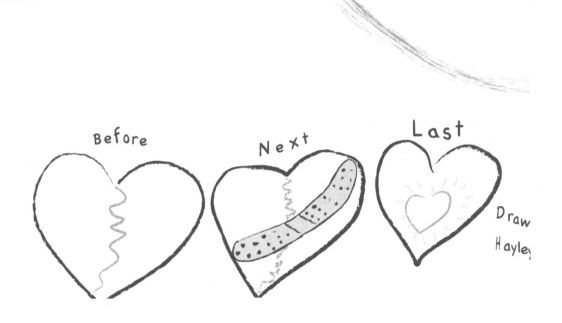

Before · Next · Last · Draw Hayley

PAUL FRIEDMAN

LESSONSFORAHAPPYMARRIAGE.COM

Published by

Orchard Concepts
3525 Del Mar Heights Rd.
San Diego, CA 92130
877-246-8596

All Rights Reserved
Copyright 2008

ISBN: 978-0-578-01749-5

Patent Pending

The Marriage Lessons contains information which has not been organized and disseminated to the general public prior to the efforts by Paul Friedman. In addition to this knowledge being based on scientifically based premises discovered by Mr. Friedman, the presentation of "Lessons for a Happy Marriage" has been presented in a specific and deliberate manner that makes comprehension and retention nearly automatic. In accordance with the governing laws of the United States of America, Mr. Friedman has been granted all practical protections provided by a provisional process patent.

Printed in U.S.A.

Contents

DEDICATION

These lessons for a Happy Marriage are dedicated to my son Joey, who is certainly in a better place but left a great void, not only in my heart and in my life, but in the hearts of all who knew him.

Simplicity Works

*I*f you pick up a pebble in your shoe and do not remove it right away, the pain will gradually build until it is unbearable. Over time, if you ignore it, a little pebble will even cause blisters and scabs. That little pebble will cause so much pain that eventually you will walk with a limp. However, once you remove the pebble, you feel immediate relief. Soon you can forget all about the pebble as your gait becomes normal and walking is a pleasure again. You also become a lot more careful about where to step, consciously avoiding pebbles. Marriage is like that. The pebbles are mistaken and unintended misbehavior that causes tremendous pain and ongoing suffering. Once you identify these destabilizing behaviors, you will have the power to avoid them.

When my wife and I were married, we had no idea the solutions for our unhappy marriage could be simple and quick. We struggled. As we individually reached the point of frustration, we turned to those we thought were the marriage experts. We went to more psychologists and family counselors than I can remember. Even though we began with faith-based renewed hope at every first visit, the happy relationship we sought never came. Even after extended periods of counseling (spanning at least ten years), any peace we reached was tense. We kept running up against the same walls, although with different wallpaper. Any calm we achieved in our relationship was short lived and fragile. Our lives were getting progressively more miserable. We openly discussed and agreed that we were staying together only for our children, but it was getting harder by the day. Finally, after twenty years, our family of five went the same way as well over 50 percent of all families in our country—it shredded in a devastating divorce.

Our children's needs are worthy of our greatest efforts

For me the pain of our divorce kept growing through many stages and phases. Although I am usually very good at figuring out what is going on, there was something too elusive for me to grasp and reconcile; it was killing me. I was confused and disoriented and I started to question if it was just me or the divorce court system (which quickly dominated our lives blocking out everything else). My first thought was that the court system was to blame for all my sorrow. After all, the divorce complex is insanely dysfunctional. It causes immediate and obvious complications that requires every ounce of attention. The horror stories I had heard about the system actually did not even come close to my own experience of the degrading and polarizing effects it had on us. I was unprepared for what we encountered. Initially I did not even notice how beaten up our kids were getting, the same ones we hung in there for! I was in complete survival mode and so was my ex.

Like most Americans, I accepted divorce as unattractive but normal. I expected a smooth transition with the help of counselors and family law experts. However, the system I discovered was completely non-user-friendly and does nothing to help parents or kids. In fact, it polarized us, the parents, completely with its crazy reward system. It added to our wounds of mistrust. Both of us had to take completely defensive postures. I was so frustrated from, and at the same time focused on, all the junk of the divorce proceedings that I did not recognize the primary cause of my suffering, which I now realize came from giving up on our marriage. At the time, I saw divorce as the only viable solution, and I assumed it would eventually all work out fine. It never did.

Divorce means inexcusable failure. I have always been successful. I take on challenges with relish. In the early seventies I began a nationally recognized food co-op. Later I started a very successful Grocery store. I have also done hands-on social work, taught, and eventually founded the largest fresh herb company in the country. With over $25 million in sales and hundreds of employees I achieved great personal success and public recognition. I founded and funded numerous humane projects of all sorts. I have always tried to help others. One of my core beliefs is "life is chiefly service." I am not a person who accepts failure, yet here it was in the one area that means the most to me: family. I had to understand what happened and do something about it.

Therefore, with a right attitude of concern but an inaccurate perspective of what divorce really signified, I became a business and family mediator.

My desire was to help others avoid the pain of the divorce system by helping divorcing couples work out separation, property, and child-raising issues without additional conflict. Good mediators can help those going through a divorce reach resolution through open discussions. I wanted to help people get out of the polarized positions they found themselves in so they could transition peacefully; at least that was my idea. The way courts value material issues such as houses and conveniences over joint parental responsibility and involvement hurts too many kids. I believed I could help people with far less wear and tears. Additionally, my long-range vision was to gain credibility as a mediator so I could do my part to help fix the system. I wanted to make it more humane; but I had not really seen the big picture yet. I was just at the tip of the real problem. I had not yet seen that divorce is completely preventable!

Fortunately though, it was not long before I noticed something very obvious. Folks who came for mediation did not really want to end their marriage at all, even when they thought they did. These good people just could not take the pressure of a dysfunctional marriage anymore and believed divorce was the only way out; just as I did. In fact, many licensed marriage counselors, including clinical psychologists who specialize in family counseling, routinely recommend divorce, incorrectly thinking it will end the pain (my ex and I also ran into one of them). It does make sense to the psychological community in a backward sort of way. How can they help people reconstruct marriage when they don't know what marriage is supposed to look like in the first place? Divorce, when recommended as a final solution in the context of helplessness, is not a bad thought. However, I was beginning to see there was a better way. God could not have made this marriage thing so difficult; we had to be the ones screwing it up.

I took a closer look at the whole marriage picture. I wanted to understand the core reasons people wanted out (and in) and see if I could help them stay together. Being a successful businessman, I knew from personal experience that **every problem can be solved once the problem is truly understood**. It became abundantly clear to me that folks who were trying to help married couples

Every problem can be solved once the problem is truly understood

simply did not understand marriage or want to admit it (the divorce statistics among marriage professionals is about the same as for the general population) so I chose to ignore faulty Western psychological theory and began a fresh search for the keys to a successful marriage. I had to reinvent the wheel without input from a system that is a proven failure.

My quest started by looking as dispassionately and objectively as I could at my own failed marriage. I had to come up with the whys. Why didn't I have a happy marriage? What did I/we do wrong? I am not stupid. My desire for happiness is as strong as could be. Neither my ex wife nor I are evil or masochistic. So what happened? It cannot be that tricky!

I explored relevant principles harvested from numerous sources regarding friendship and loyalty in order to gain a broader perspective. I concluded that **active friendship is a cornerstone of sound marital relationships**. I wanted to understand friendship because marriage is the greatest friendship opportunity most of us will ever have.

Next, I created a "happy marriage" template, a schematic design of positive interactions, as well as the corresponding potential pitfalls and subsequent temptations. This was the easy part. Visualizing harmonious living is not that difficult for any of us. I just had to figure out why living it was so tough. I drew a "picture" of a happy marriage and placed it next to my past marriage so I could clearly compare the differences. It was brutal but necessary. I wanted peace; we had tension and arguments. I wanted trust, caring, support, intimacy, and love. Instead, every petty problem eclipsed what I wanted. I asked myself the pertinent questions and a conceptual understanding started to take shape in my mind. I jotted down some assumptions and equations of cause and effect, which I randomly tested informally with various individuals, including my then current clients. I also experimented during my own interactions; studying people's reactions to my words and behaviors. I had to be sure I didn't become another irrelevant theorist. I wanted my conceptual understanding to become realistic and practical, so I tested everything from every angle I could imagine. Over time, my view of marriage began to take definite shape and make a lot of sense. It was, ultimately, simple; and because it was coming up simple, I knew I was on the right track.

I had to test my newfound knowledge on real-life desperate marriage cases, the more hopeless the better for these purposes. If my cures worked on the hopeless, they would work on everyone. Helping couples who only needed a little encouragement would do nothing to prove any process. My thinking is if it is broken big or broken little the fix should be the same and work either way. I did not want to leave room in my mind for rationalizations and excuses that could undermine my goal of true understanding and reliable results.

Once a malfunctioning "part" is replaced it can cause no more damage; big or little

I had no qualms about experimenting with real people. I had heard a story on PBS about marriage counseling that reported the success rate for Western psychologists was below 6 percent; I was shocked (none of the counselors we saw ever admitted failure—it was always vaguely our fault). Can you imagine any repairperson (we expected our therapists to help us *repair* our marriage) with that kind of failure rate calling themselves an expert? I knew I wouldn't do that poorly.

I did not work with people who thought I was something I am not. Everyone knew going in that my efforts were experimental and nonintrusive, not therapeutic or diagnostic. I was very clear that I was a mediator and not a student of Western psychology or a professional anything other than a mediator. I would explain marriage and help them compare; they would fix.

Complete success is the only reasonable goal

I created an outline for a tutorial and shifted my mediation focus to help folks get back together instead of divorce. My goal of complete success included designing a transparent process that suggested a few simple commonsense steps that individuals would need to take toward their own success, and how to take those steps quickly. My clients were given realistic timelines for that success (the whole process got down to three two-hour weekly sessions, on the outside). I made an outline on my whiteboard to address the main points. People knew the path to take and the milestones they could expect along the way. To avoid the common and deflating expectation of long, drawn-out and painful processes, I made it clear I would give all their money back if we were unsuccessful. My motivation was to prove my goal was realistic based on real-life success. I also burned the bridge behind me; I refused to help any more folks get a divorce.

In less than two years I unearthed almost every nuance of all the important lessons they had to learn. As I encountered the

Forget the past and focus on what you can do to improve your relationship right now

same questions from my clients I was able to adjust the emphasis to tougher-to-learn points. My tutorial became consistent and the positive outcomes predictable. I even came to the point where I could usually tell if a couple needed to hear the whole "shebang" in great technical detail or just needed a little nudge and reminder. In a few cases I could show a person the way on the phone in our preliminary discussion. If a pebble is plucked early, it is not as damaging.

These lessons contain all you will need. While writing this, I often passed on the near-completed manuscript to new acquaintances who needed useful guidance with their marriage to test the effectiveness of the lessons in written form. Here is an example of typical feedback:

Hi Paul,

I want to thank you for sending me your book. I am about half way through and it has immediately impacted my life. I explained to my wife, Lori, our meeting and the book and she has just about completed it. . . .

I am not a very religious person but I do believe in divine intervention.

I am beginning to believe our chance meeting just wasn't that, chance. . . .

I can't begin to tell you how much I appreciate what you had shared with me/us. Our marriage is now on the right track of recovery. When I met you on Friday, I literally thought my marriage was done. Now it is not even a thought in my mind.

Again, thank you and if I run into you at Starbucks I owe you a coffee . . . it's the least I can do.

Brad

This e-mail was not edited in any way, shape, or form. They are normal—like you. These people went from despair and inevitable divorce to understanding as quickly as it took to read the lessons; in hours.

If you are in a troubled marriage use this knowledge to quickly end the suffering. You will learn how to move beyond the hurt. You will learn to behave in a way that creates joy and security. Those of you in new marriages will see that marriage is wonderful when you understand it. Everything in these lessons will teach you what you need to know. You can succeed when it all makes sense. There is no hocus pocus or new age pontifications that will give you temporary good feelings. This works because it is clear from beginning to end. This is a reliable manual. It works, when applied, immediately—now. It is not complicated either. Your marriage is quickly fixable!

Your success will come very fast Don't take too long to accept it

Marriages that end in divorce are rarely lost because of insurmountable issues such as complete mental instability, which leads to physical danger and/or other radical problems. Commonly perceived *big* issues like infidelity, mistrust, loss of respect, financial problems, and emotional suffering are actually symptoms of one or more of the three killers thrust upon people who have no idea what they are doing to themselves and each other. The so-called big issues are forgivable and forgettable when understood in proper context. Couples learn why and how to move on.

Don't your kids deserve all the effort you can make?

Obviously there are relationships in which, sadly, one or both partners fall so far that they are abusive by any standard. Threatening conditions cannot be taken lightly. Each of us must take personal responsibility for our children's safety and our own. I did not work with couples who lived with physical violence or drug (including alcohol) abuse. Neither did I work with couples where one partner did not want to participate, or where there was a serious psychological disorder. These lessons definitely work for those who want to stay married but need the "manual". They also work for others who have "gone crazy" because of the pressures caused by mutual misbehaviors, You will know if you try.

I hope current trendy rationalizations that try to convince you your kids will do fine when their home is broken do not fool you. Kids do not do fine at all. They adapt, but so what? My father and many like him adapted to concentration camps. That is not doing fine. It is noble to be willing to hang in there for the kids, but I do not advocate a life of suffering. I advocate marriage filled with joy. When you make your marriage into something truly wonderful, everyone wins. Isn't it how it is supposed to be, where everyone

Marriage is meant to be joyous— never a struggle

wins? I know many of you good people are hanging in there for the sake of your children. I praise you! Now is the time to get the joy back into your marriage so your kids will not be the only reason to be married. Your children will benefit when you are happily married. What a difference! Please do not entertain the notion that your best hope is a marriage that you can 'live with.' You will have a marriage you will not want to live without.

I met with some people who believed they already lost a marriage they did not want to lose. Some already moved out and/or had begun the legal process of divorce; I was their last shot, like the cancer clinics in Mexico. Do not give up! Ninety-nine percent of the time both partners make the effort after a bit, but mutual agreement is not a prerequisite for happiness. You can lead the way. Yes, you will have to make changes but only changes that make sense to you. After twenty minutes of their first session, it was obvious to couples that these lessons work. The proof is in the pudding, and you will see. Once you understand the underlying principles, correct behavior is obvious, which it should be. I never listen to people's issues and "whodunwhats." There is no need for therapy or dispute resolution. When you bring your car to the shop after running around with a flat front tire, it doesn't help the mechanic change the tire if you go on and on about how the car pulls, loses traction, how you skid, or all the other likely results of driving a car with a flat. Changing the tire is all it takes. There is nothing mystical or magical. The lessons work because it explains and illustrates the mechanical principles of a happy marriage relationship. All advice is solution-oriented. The expected result is a happy marriage.

It was not the good fortune of my family to have this knowledge when we were married, or we would still be married. On the other hand, I never would have produced these lessons without the painful prod of my own losses. God bless your family!

For most, these lessons work fast and easily
For some, it requires more effort to change bad habits.
Go for it!
You can do it!

One more thing: Learn these lessons as conceptually as you can. Don't get hung up on every word or detail. There are different ways of hearing things. This book contains more information than any particular couple received in a session. My goal is to get you going in the right direction as efficiently as possible. You will not hear it all even if you read it all; neither will you need to. You will hear what you are ready to hear, and it will be enough.

Additionally, everything is presented in a very definite order, so don't skip around until you have finished the book once. There is a compounding of knowledge that comes from reading the lessons in the order I wrote them. Definitely, do not read the last chapter, on intimacy, until you have assimilated the foundational principles built one upon the other in the previous chapters. Now smile; you are embarking on a new and wonderful beginning.

Make a list of your spouse's good qualities.

Now pretend you are their lawyer. It is up to you to convince a jury that your spouse is a good person. Elaborate on each quality to save your spouse from a crime they did not commit. It is all up to you. You are the only one who will speak up for your spouse. You must do a great job. Go beyond your own ability. Be incredible.

Now understand that this is how you are supposed to feel and think and speak about your spouse all the time.

Whenever negative thoughts about your spouse rise in your mind recall your pitch to the jury and re-pitch yourself.

Simplicity works. If something sounds complicated you have possibly misread it. A perfect marriage is the only reasonable goal for anyone.

Lesson Exercise

The Three Marriage Killers

*T*he first thing you will want to do is stop hurting each other. . . . agreed?

When you learned to drive a car, which is actually more complicated than creating a successful marriage, the first thing you learn are the don'ts. Don't drive on the wrong side of the road, don't drink and drive, don't accelerate in unsafe conditions, and don't get mad at other drivers; just mind your own driving business. Some cautions are blatantly obvious while others are only obvious after a brief explanation. Some complex don'ts, however, need to be explained in more detail, or just accepted; like not hitting the brakes during a skid even though it is a normal and instinctive reaction.

The don'ts in marriage warn about the "killers." Paying attention to the don'ts will work. Once revealed, you can remember them when you see them popping in and stop dangerous thoughts and deeds. The problem is you have not known what the don'ts are (they really should teach this stuff in school). The don'ts you do will often overwhelm all the good you have already done. They eclipse your loving and positive behavior (which might now seem almost absent to your spouse after the buildup of pain). Marriage has no tally sheet where you get to balance your good and bad. There is no scorecard. The bad blocks views of the good no matter how vast the good is, just as your hand can completely block the entire sun from your view. Even though both of you are really good people with your good traits far outweighing your bad habits, it is hard to feel it because of the eclipse effect; like when a tiny part on your car goes out and the whole car shakes like a jalopy. This is a good thing. Because just as fixing one small part will have you driving a great car again, or moving your hand away from your eyes will open you to the world, so removing the little bad habits that are undermining your marital happiness will allow the innate joy of marriage to fill your lives again.

The three "killers" become like roots that produce various evil vines and destructive fruits. In order to kill all the fruit and vines, one must attack only the roots. By putting most of your attention on the first killer (which is the biggest and most fundamental to your problems) you will surely succeed. The rest will fall into place. God did not invent marriage to make you suffer. You are entitled to the results that automatically come from well-defined and purposeful actions of beneficially oriented behavior. So take control and start cultivating the relationship you have always wanted.

The Three Killers (Pebbles) of Marriage

1. Overfamiliarity

2. Poor Communication

3. "Business Arrangement" Mentality
(Rare, but most lethal)

Overfamiliarity

Overfamiliarity means you are taking each other for granted; you have become, in a word, disrespectful if not downright mean. Overfamiliarity will destroy every relationship all by itself; it is *deadly*! Being disrespectful to your spouse is like smiling at them while you slap them silly. Marrying your spouse sent a message of acceptance (the smile). Disrespectfulness is the slap. It is not the deadliest killer, since it is the killer most easily fixed, but it is by far the biggest killer because it is at the bottom of *every* hurting marriage. Don't be over-familiar. If you learn how and why the terrible habit of disrespectfulness is able to take root in the first place, you can nip it in the bud whenever it tries to sneak in.

Behaving *respectfully* and lovingly toward your spouse is the first rule to follow for ending all the pain. When you first met, you treated each other with kind and cautious respect, which is always normal when meeting someone new. Then when you saw the potential for marriage, you both began to ratchet up your attractiveness by making progressively greater effort to show each other your best side; this was good! You were patient, kind, and attentive. You were sweet, funny, considerate, noble, and appreciative (right?). You were oh-so-polite, always smiling, always complimenting each other, and you laughed at each other's jokes even when they were not that funny. You dressed to impress, washed behind your ears, and bent over backward to do special little things for each other; you bought flowers, made cookies, maybe called each other all the time. You treated your "squeeze" correctly! You may laugh when you recall doing some of the things you did to ensure that you were the kind of person who would

Start behaving respectfully again

impress your crush. They were not crazy things; you wanted your crush to appreciate you and love you enough to choose you as the "one."

You were trying to win each other's love and respect. Perfect!
Start doing so again.

Trying to impress your pre-spouse was not phony! It was practical. You exposed the real you instead of the unattractive habits you thought might be a turn-off. What is wrong with that! **Your habits are not you.**

It is smart to be considerate and create new habits that make you happy. You behave well towards any person who is important to you. You are at your best anytime acceptance is important to you. Your spouse's acceptance of your flaws was and is not a grace you should think of as a "given." You are not automatically entitled to acceptance even though you need to give unconditional acceptance yourself. Do you recall when your pre-spouse was in a bad mood or had a bad day and you did all you could to ease their suffering? That is correct behavior! You did not expect them to "come around" or "snap out of it." You were authentically concerned only for them rather than how they might be bumming you out. You probably didn't even think of them as bumming you out because you put them ahead of yourself. Expecting unconditional acceptance is selfish, whereas giving it is correct.

After some time you became over-familiar with your spouse and stopped behaving at basic levels of consideration. It became all about you. Can you recall the last time you thought about what would really make your spouse happy? You take your spouse for granted, and resentment has become the normal response to his or her needs. Perhaps you see your spouse's needs as an imposition on you. Most people do wish to serve their spouses, but I have never met anyone who wanted to be abused. Many women occasionally enjoy the fantasy of being a courtesan, but no woman wants to be treated like a whore. Most men take pride in doing "honey-dos" for their wives, but none wish to be the house slave. Instead of treating each other like royalty forever, as you promised, you fell into habits of behavior you would never dare use on anyone else. What

You define who you are by how you behave. Blaming your behavior on how someone treats you really defines your own weaknesses, not the other person's violations.

happened to the flowers? What happened to the smiles and sexy looks? What happened to compliments, sweet phone messages, careful grooming, supportive chats, little gifts, funny stories, gentle smooches, loving looks, special dinners, unasked for shoulder rubs? They have gone out the window. You replaced good and appropriate behavior with sarcastic comments, critical thoughts, commands, insults, complaints, nagging, and unfair expectations. I mean, c'mon! When you enter someone's space with rudeness, anger, criticism, expectations, and other destructiveness, you are offensive; you are being overly familiar. Do you really expect your spouse to cherish you when you are mean in return? Even a sweet dog will eventually bite you if you mistreat it every day. Do you think you now know each other well enough to treat each other without consideration? Do you believe you have reached a point when it becomes okay to be a jerk? Is that what friendship is supposed to evolve into? No way! You have traded the bliss that comes from consistent loving behavior for the perverse right to speak your mind and act out your most lowbrow behaviors.

Go back to your sweet behavior even if your spouse does not. It is your job to try to win your spouse's affection and appreciation—regardless of how you are treated.

I have heard so many variations of "it's different when you're married." Yes, it is *supposed* to be different; different better! **The more you know your friend and lover, the more you are supposed to use your intimate knowledge to be nicer in ways that no one else in the world can match because no one knows the little secrets about your spouse like you.** Instead you unthinkingly behave in a way that says, because you are married you may abuse each other as if that is what you and your spouse signed up for.

You did not did not sign up for abuse!

Your spouse did not sign up for abuse!

Isn't this so unbelievably simple? Do not follow the ways of the world. It does not work. Stop being mean. Replace the over-familiar behavior with great behavior and make extra good behavior a habit. Don't you want to be treated the way you were treated when you were courting? Would you consider marrying the person who treats you the way you are currently treated? Well, neither would your spouse.

> **Treat your spouse as if they are the most important person you have ever met; they are**

You are supposed to take advantage of the security of the marriage contract by opening your heart and expressing love without inhibition. Express loyalty and appreciation like you ought to. (Don't care or worry if your spouse does not get this. Just do what *you* are supposed to do.)

Predicate your behavior on what you know to be right rather than how others, your spouse included, behave. You are ultimately responsible for only your own behavior. This point is critical to the success of your marriage. If you wait for your spouse to measure up before you take the next step, you will fail. Behaving well toward a person who does not treat you as you desire is a sign of maturity. No time limits and no conditions should interfere with your efforts to behave well. You are hurting each other and have become so used to it that you do not see how mean and ugly you have become. You do not hear yourself when you speak to your spouse. Your meanness in whatever form it comes was extremely painful in the beginning before you became numb. Perhaps it is still painful, but you hardly notice it through the anger and hurt.

Life is not like a TV sitcom where it is funny or entertaining to be vicious or sarcastic. It is not comical to judge or ridicule another's weakness or unfortunate predicament and goof on them. Nor is it your right to notice your spouse's flaws or behavioral faux pas. It is time to stop this atrocious behavior right now! I have heard so many exceptions. They are not valid. There is never a justifiable reason to be mean or inconsiderate; excuses are a form of lying.

You have no right, no matter what the circumstances, to criticize your partner. Not only is criticism simply an expression of your own shortcomings but it never, never, never achieves your desired result, immediate or long term.

If you see your spouse doing something wrong, which is anything you don't happen to like, just stop your own mind from judging and think about changing your own behavior, or dwell upon one of the many positive traits your spouse has. Take note of your own behavior without comparing it to your spouse. Marriage is not a contest. It is a codependent independent team. If your spouse has difficulty living up to standards you have set for him or her, the real problem is that you are being judgmental. Do you see what I mean? Support your spouse at every turn.

Start being kind now. Stop being critical now. Stop saying things that are offensive and disrespectful. *Say things that are complimentary and gracious.* Gracious means something your spouse will like hearing. If you stop being mean and start being kind, everything will immediately improve. You have the power!

Only one couple I worked with told me they treated each other well. They were just numb. After some challenging discussions, they began to see how much they abused each other in subtle ways. Subtle attacks and hurts cause not so subtle pain and resentment. Because this couple remained *polite*, they thought they were nice.

"Insincerity is like a beautiful dead lady." Being polite just to be polite is only slightly better than remaining quiet. However, it is better to start with politeness than to wait until you *feel* like being polite. You must refocus on your love and build it again in your heart and actions. Tend to this precious plant without applying "lovicides" of inconsiderate behavior. Make your mind return to the thoughts that will benefit your relationship by making your spouse feel loved and appreciated.

Not long ago I went for coffee with a couple of my friends (women), one married and the other divorced. Grace asked Lilly about her marriage, and Lilly started to tell us the good . . . and the bad. I told Lilly that she was breaking a cardinal rule. One must never say anything that can be even remotely construed as negative about their spouse. (Are you guilty of this, too?)

Lilly said she was just being truthful, and I complimented her for her intention. I reminded her that her intention to be loyal must supersede all other intentions. I suggested if her husband heard what she said he would probably be hurt, and she agreed. I also let her know that **giving hurtful facts about someone is not being truthful** because the mind of the listener will always fixate on the negative and have an unbalanced and thus untruthful understanding of the person whose character is being discussed. Think how challenging it is to remain positive about a friend you hear gossip about even though most of your previous experience with that person is positive. When we listen to someone going on about someone's flaws, we are all ears. Some say it is human nature, but in reality it is a learned response, a destructive habit that needs to change.

Both listening to gossip and speaking gossip are horrible and we all know it. Can you see how gossiping about your own spouse

Never allow a negative thought, word or deed to be entertained about your spouse.

Be their greatest fan club at all times; that is love as a verb.

Assume the virtue of being the world's greatest spouse until you are

because you are mad over some trifle of the moment is traitorous? Is this cool? It is so accepted as normal these days! Other people I have met with said they only put down their spouse to a close confidant; they said they needed to speak to someone or they might explode. Explode then! Why would you give ammunition to someone about your own spouse, your best friend, your soul mate, your precious love? It is all too common to take for granted the person we are closest to (the definition of irony!). We actually feel privileged to be the one who can inform others of otherwise hidden flaws. That's not nice! But it is easy to change this habit to the opposite habit of praising your spouse. Change now! Be utterly respectful of your spouse at all times, whether or not you are in each other's presence.

The current thinking is you ought to have compassionate understanding about the flaws of others. We rationalize away flaws by not judging them and talk about them as neutral observers. We use imagined or real excuses to explain away evil. I am not asking you to do that because it diminishes your natural repulsion toward evil behavior. Evil should be exposed so that it can be eradicated. You need to catch your evil, not others'. Let your spouse and others work on their own flaws. Unfortunately the mind prefers to notice the flaws of others, especially your spouse's, because it feels comforted to see the cause of its suffering as something outside of your own thinking and behavior so your mind won't feel pressure to change its comfortable bad habits (which requires some courage and effort to change).

You did not get married to work on each other's flaws

Remember that other people's evil is their problem and nothing you say or do can get them to change. Any effort you make toward changing them is effort not made toward changing your own evil habits, which compounds your error. In addition, pointing out your loved one's flaws is the opposite of loving behavior. You must see your spouse as the most beautiful or handsome person you have ever seen. Don't go along with the Hollywood version of beauty. Go along with your heart's version.

1. **Can you control or change your spouse's mind (or behavior)? Answer: NO way**
2. **Can your spouse control or change your mind (or behavior)? Answer: NOPE**
3. **Do you try to control and change your spouse? Answer: Of course you do!**

Yes, you do! You can protest if you want, but nearly everyone tries to control his or her spouse. **Trying to control your spouse in small or big ways is both offensive and useless.**

Everyone who is uninformed tries to get his or her spouse to change. Trying to change your spouse is a losing proposition for both of you. This is the part about braking when your car is in a skid; you will crash if you try, even though it seems to be the right thing to do. Try to change your spouse and you will crash. The mind comes up with many rationalizations and exceptions, so we must stick to our commitment to mind our own business, to change only ourselves. It is an absolute!

The mere subconscious desire to blame and change outer circumstances (i.e., our spouse's behavior or thinking) leads to nothing but frustration for everyone. Life is much sweeter when we refuse to try to change each other even when asked. When we learn to appreciate instead of criticize each other and change flaws we see in ourselves, we become much more fun. Avoid giving advice even when begged. There are much better ways to be helpful.

Face it; it is easier to notice flaws in others. **All logic dictates the futility of trying to change another person. We will not allow another person to change us, yet we actually think they will be grateful for our advice.** Our habits push us into this ridiculous behavior. It is so common; this flawed behavior is not seen as flawed behavior in our society, so we bang our heads against the same wall repeatedly and then wonder what is wrong with the other person. Why don't they change? We see it everywhere. Everyone is always criticizing everyone else, blaming everyone or anything else when something is not how he or she wants it to be. It is an epidemic in this world—an epidemic of a disease called over-familiarity. Though we hate it when someone blames us, even when we accidentally did something wrong, we think nothing of blaming someone else for whatever unfortunate event might befall us. It's crazy!

We usually blame the person we are supposed to love with all our hearts. Moreover, it is always for the most petty and unanticipated things. Do you see the irony? **The one person we vow to love, cherish, respect, and hold dear is the one who gets our unrestricted crap. It is insane!**

Your spouse is just fine as they are (no one is perfect)

Don't try to change them or even convince them of something... just listen and learn

Overfamiliarity needs to be replaced with unconditional respect. Honor your spouse. Your happy marriage will bounce back faster than you can imagine. Your marriage relationship is organic, and it will heal very quickly when you stop the bad behavior—when you remove the pebbles.

Apologize to your spouse even if he or she cannot hear you. Ask for forgiveness. Promise you will try never to be mean again. Don't allow your mind to think your spouse does it so you can to do it too. Finding excuses is the greatest pitfall to success. It can be insidious. Most people see this flawed behavior in their spouse without realizing judgemental thoughts must never be entertained in their own mind.

You should not allow critical thoughts to sprout into disrespectful behavior. Kick those thoughts out! Control your words and behavior. Control the mind. It is *your* mind, and you can control it. When you first met, you were respectful because you feared rejection. That's a fine reason! Whatever you need to motivate your good behavior is fine. That particular fear can be healthy. Of course it's better to behave well because you wish to please your spouse, but I'll take the fear motivator over mean treatment any time.

Try hard to stop yourself from thinking or saying things like, "I knew you would do that," or "you never listen to me," or "I saw that coming." Allow only kind and beneficial thoughts about your spouse to be expressed in your behavior and words. Assuming the positive instead of the negative is very important.

When was the last time you dwelled on good thoughts about your spouse? Think of some right now. Really! Right now.

When was the last time you couldn't stop thinking about how good a person your spouse is or how much you love him/her? Do it now!

Make it a habit to be your spouse's most ardent supporter. That is what loyalty means.

If you do your part, you will have a great marriage; even if your spouse does not do his or her part, such is the power of right behavior.

Have you, perhaps, lost your objectivity? Obviously. When you were courting each other, you saw only the good qualities and barely noticed the little flaws. Now is the time to stop the evil thoughts about your spouse that ruin your day. Replace them with sweet thoughts. You can relive those dreamy courting days by controlling your mind and behavior.

Some people actually believe, "if only I had a better partner everything would be fine." While they are married they look around for the so-called perfect partner by looking at the surface of others—looks, easy demeanors, and other image traits—then become more negative toward their spouse. They do not realize that in the beginning people show only the good just as they did.

The surface does not tell the whole story. When you switch partners, you only switch mirrors and your same bad traits will show up again until you get rid of them. I tell you this so that you will stop comparing your spouse with others and you get started making the *tiny* effort of controlling your own behavior instead; I say *tiny* in comparison with the guaranteed gargantuan suffering that comes from ignoring this reality.

When you recognize how much poison you have been spewing into your relationship and stop, you will have won half the battle. **Evil thoughts, feelings, and speech are erosive toxins eating away your relationship as surely as acid eats away the most durable steel.** Another self-interested way to look at this is to recognize your thoughts as your closest environment; even closer than the nose on your face. You live in the "mental" environment you create. When your thoughts and feelings are miserable, you live in a self-created miserable environment. When you make sure your thoughts and feelings are positive and uplifting, or compassionate and charitable, you live in a healthy mental environment. It's completely up to you. As this concept sinks in, **your relationship already improves, because the relationship will heal when it is not subjected to those things that are destroying it—the pebbles of inadvertent misbehavior.**

You didn't mean to become mean. Of course, the options are yours. You don't have to follow this practical advice; it is *your* call. You can imagine that someone else created your suffering if you want to. You have free will and will do whatever you want, but has it *ever* worked when you tried to change your spouse? If they chose to go along with your demands when you were insistent, did it really help for long, or did you just keep noticing new flaws to make yourself miserable?

Marrying the "wrong" person is extremely rare. Focus only on the good traits of your spouse.

You didn't mean to become mean.

You can control a great deal in your life and learn about whom you really are by learning to control your own mind. If you make the effort to control what you are able to control—your mind—you will be happy. Stop banging your head against the wall. Stop trying to control or change your spouse.

Stop expecting.

Stop manipulating.

Stop asking for this or that.

Summary

The greatest expression of overfamiliarity is to get into someone else's space with judgment and criticism. Instead, always compliment your spouse. Always compliment your spouse. No matter what your mind is thinking, all you have to do is shift your thinking and deliver a sweet compliment. You won't lose a thing, but you will gain much. Always compliment your spouse.

Quiz

Fill in the blanks.

1. I will never _____ my spouse again.

2. I will always look for opportunities to _____ my spouse.

Answers: 1. criticize; 2. compliment

The recurring associated theme is to look at your own stuff, which is all you need to be concerned with in order to find happiness and meaning in your life. Graciously allow other people the space to grow and develop when and if they choose.

Highly evolved people don't try to force growth or change on others (except their kids) because it doesn't work. They work only on themselves and never consider another person's flaws; they realize that only their own flaws bring pain. At the same time they diplomatically and lovingly support the positive efforts of those who wish to change.

Great prophets of every religion demonstrate unconditional love and commitment to our salvation. They never attempt to beat us into right behavior. They inspire us by their own right behavior—it's a free-will game. We have no right to try to change another person; especially not our spouse!

Men and women often express overfamiliarity differently The following is not an attempt to cover all expressions of overfamiliarity, just a way to get you to recognize some of your own undesirable expressions. See if some of these behaviors are part of your own repertoire. Consider if they are respectful and loving or if they should be removed.

Men

- Belching or worse (you know what I mean) in front of your wife
- Leaving the toilet seat up
- Discourteous speech such as swearing
- Expressing anger verbally or otherwise
- Expressing impatience
- Looking at other women
- Flirting and/or responding to flirtatiousness
- Expecting sex as if from a prostitute
- Not defending your wife from attacks
- Not understanding her point of view
- Having mean or degrading thoughts about your wife
- Trying to control the finances
- Trying to control your wife's behavior
- Making fun of your wife, even "jokingly"
- Criticizing your wife
- Assuming you know what she is thinking

There are many more ways, but I hope I have made my point and you can think of ways in which you have stopped treating your wife with the same level of respect you want for yourself. On the other hand, if you are a wife, you will be reading this and thinking, "Uh huh, that's what he does!" If you are having thoughts about his flaws, you are, unfortunately, doing more than acknowledging a situation; you are being critical and thus expressing a form of

List the ways you have become over-familiar

disrespect. Do not take flawed behavior from your spouse as a personal attack. In most cases, the insults are not intentionally aimed at you. If you assume they are intentional or loaded, you will make yourself a victim. Being a victim is a personal choice.

Women

- Having unkind thoughts about your husband
- Talking unfavorably about your husband to your friends (so commonly accepted, and so horrible)
- Not considering family budgets
- Dumping emotionally on your husband
- Unkind speech such as nagging
- Ordering him instead of asking
- Letting your body go (This is a sensitive topic. It has to do with caring about pleasing him. The idea of "if he doesn't like me the way I am . . ." is not the point. Nor are we looking for 100 percent compliance in any of these examples. This is a reminder that your intentions have shifted from a desire to please to destructive apathy or resentment.)
- Criticizing your husband openly and in private
- Reading your husband's mind
- Finishing his thoughts and sentences
- Not demonstrating love and loyalty through intimacy (well covered in the last lesson)
- Manipulatively withholding affection
- Blaming your husband for misunderstandings
- Taking sides with children or others publicly
- Interrupting his train of thought with your own ideas
- Unilaterally changing the subject

Entertaining unkind thoughts about your spouse undermines your marriage

There are many ways you currently express disrespectfulness that sprouts from overfamiliarity. I hope you will see that over-familiar behavior is not conducive to a harmonious and loving relationship. If you and your husband treated one another in an unloving manner when you were courting, there is not a chance you would have chosen to marry each other, The same point can be made to men. If you are thinking, "Yes, she does all that and more," then you are being critical. You need to think something along the lines of, "My lovely wife may have a few flaws, but I refuse to notice them; they are so small compared to all the wonderful traits I see. I love her so much."

The main point is *both* individuals have stopped treating each other with the love and respect expressed during courting. You are cheating yourselves out of what you rightfully expected from marriage. I will address this in more detail a bit later, but the main point is neither of you are happy with how you are treated and one or both of you may be blaming the other for "starting it." Therefore, I ask you now at this very moment to make a conscious effort to recognize only your own misbehavior and take responsibility for being kind, regardless of how you are being treated.

Yes, that is correct: **No matter how you are being treated, I am asking you to be kind, courteous, and well behaved.** Stop lowering yourself by imagining you would behave better if your spouse did. You behave the way you choose when you control your mind. Just do it because it makes sense. Everyone will like you better; but that doesn't matter! **Be kind because you know it's the right thing to do.**

It's not what is wrong with your spouse that is the problem with your marriage. Your spouse is merely the catalyst for revealing your own flaws. Your behavior is a reflection of how you wish to live. Treat your spouse better than *anyone else* in the world no matter how your spouse treats you, even if it appears unfair at the moment.

How you behave is what you are. One of my favorite stories emphasizes this point. This story is true, as far as I know.

Though suffering in a concentration camp, an inmate was saying a prayer of thanksgiving. His friend, overhearing this well-known prayer, was startled by his friend's prayers of sincere and humble gratitude and asked, "How can you be grateful? Have you lost your mind? You have lost everything else! You are skin and bones, your family is dead, all is gone and you are dying! What can you possibly be thankful for?"

His friend softly answered, "I am grateful that God didn't make me like those who put us in here."

> **Do what you should do, not what you want to do**

You do not need to be perfect to be happily married.

The wise man in this story was not allowing his outer circumstances to control his self-view or his behavior. His noble attitude removed him from the victim designation despite every outward circumstance, so he was not compelled to retaliate. In his mind, he was a free man who felt joy because he did not let anyone or anything interfere with his lofty attitude. He reframed his perspective of the situation to demonstrate his inner peace rather than his outer temporary agonies. What he did you can do also! It's not as hard as it seems; it is a matter of training the mind to respond in ways that give you joy instead of sorrow. It's all up to you. Ultimately, you are a victim only if you choose to be one by seeing yourself compromised.

Don't waste your effort on changing your spouse; change how you perceive your spouse. That doesn't mean you should become a fatalist. I am not asking you to be a doormat either. On the contrary, when you control your mind, you are the master of your destiny. Circumstances will change with the right effort, but the effort put into changing yourself is the most useful effort of all. The effort you make will guarantee you will be a happier person no matter what the situation. It is the effort itself that pays off. You do not need to be perfect to be happily married. Just remember never to criticize and always praise.

Remember, you chose your spouse to be your lover, best friend, co-parent, business partner, and more. You chose this person for the rest of your life. You weren't crazy or ill-informed. You just didn't know how to behave in a relationship and now you are learning these things; everything will work out.

Years ago, the Thames River in England was pronounced dead. It was so polluted that there were no more fish in it. The government passed strong laws and made cleaning the river a national cause. Everybody got on board because the pollution impacted their lives in ugly ways. Within a short time, to the amazement of all the skeptics the river came back and is now clean and sweet. No one had to sanitize the waters or re-filter it. They just stopped polluting. Stop polluting your marriage, and soon you will be drinking the nectar of a loving marriage with your soul mate.

Ask yourself what your most destructive trait is; write it down on a piece of paper you can carry with you. Every time you catch your mind going there and don't act on it give yourself a point. When you don't catch it and you act out, take a point away.

The two best ways to eliminate bad habits are by using sheer will power to deny the unwanted habit (I refuse to be angry) and by replacing the bad habit with the opposite good habit (I am feeling angry so I will be sympathetic). Strong habits take stronger resolve. Pernicious habits can be overcome. Never give up!

Communication

*M*ost individuals reach the point where they are afraid to open their mouths for fear of saying something that will trigger a war or get a negative or condescending response. Men are paranoid about asking for sex. On the other side of the same coin, women are afraid to express any physical affection because they fear (know) it will lead to demands for sex. Eventually men stop asking and some wives then wonder why they are not desired. Although at first this seemed like a communication problem to virtually every couple I met with, this particular dilemma is actually about intimacy. My reason for bringing it up first even though it's not, at its core, a communication problem is to assure you that this common problem is thoroughly addressed in the chapter on intimacy. (Please, don't skip ahead!).

Communication is very powerful.

Be careful how you use it.

Never say mean things.

Always speak lovingly and listen supportively.

Communication is a delivery system. How and what you deliver should correctly fit the venue and circumstances. Marital communication is unique because you should primarily be trying (like 98 percent or more) to deliver *love and support* to your spouse. Additionally, how you communicate with your spouse must be more respectful and courteous than with anyone else. The principle of *expressed* mutual adoration is the common denominator in every happy marriage.

Expressed mutual adoration is the common denominator in every happy marriage

It is ALWAYS the right time to compliment or praise your spouse

Most couples having marital problems use communication strictly to achieve their own ends instead of serving the needs of their spouses. For example, it is hurtful to "not really listen" to your spouse (whether you are assuming you know what is coming or you are just waiting until you can get your ideas out because you think they are of greater value). It is vitally important to think of your mate as an equal you love to love, and communicate with him or her with all the respect and consideration possible.

Learn the principles and rules for marital communication, which are quite simple and natural. They make perfect sense for how one should treat one's best friend and soul mate. Because the purpose and rules for marital communication differ significantly from other types of communication, sound principles that are completely effective in other venues will cause tension and misunderstanding in a marital relationship (all car wheels seem about the same until you put the wrong size wheel on your car). For instance, proving your ideas are correct may win you a promotion at work, or more security in your job, but proving you were right at home will ruin your plans for a loving evening.

Most folks are great communicators at work and expect appreciation at home by using the same methods. On the job, you depend on each other for your living so you are more or less obligated to do your best; there is not much wiggle room or much forgiveness for breaches of workplace etiquette. Good communication skills in the workplace, therefore, are more accurately termed survival skills. The threat of "consequences" if you do not perform well is inherent in the work place relationship, so everybody stays consciously alert. In contrast, **most people incorrectly assume they can say what they want and how they say it in their marriage** (due to overfamiliarity and ignorance of the ramifications). This unfortunate assumption leads to a lot of hurt feelings.

It is NEVER the right time to criticize or challenge your spouse

Marriage communication is as different from work place and other communication as could be. First and uniquely, the goal of communication in marriage is primarily to express love and support. The ongoing business items in your marriage (as opposed to being the driving force in a business environment) are of far less importance than enjoying the love and security you envisioned (and still need) when you chose to marry. If you list by order of importance the desires you wish to fulfill in marriage, I am certain that deciding who is responsible for taking out the trash will not be high on the list. Most people allow their emotional state to drive up the seeming importance of things and lose a lot of peace; so keep things in perspective.

The goal of communication in marriage is primarily to *express* **love and support.** No matter what the momentary purpose for communicating may be, if you remember this principle you will get the most out of your relationship. The connection that you want and need with each other will fall into place because you will communicate what is important. You got married in order to have a partner who loves you and supports you. Your spouse got married for the same reason. Do not be lured into thinking something might be so "important" that this principle takes a momentary back seat. Continuously demonstrate to your spouse how important she or he is by how and what you communicate. You might as well face life's business items with your lover by your side instead of in your face. The bottom line is to remember to be supportive and loving at *all* times, no matter what—just like when you first started dating. Progressively applying the right rules will progressively improve your life.

There are useful don'ts and dos that support the principles in these lessons:

- **Don't be mean (from your spouse's point of view, so pay attention to their reactions).** It is very easy to allow emotions (yours or theirs) to control your mouth and mind. Begin a conscious effort to be absolutely in control of what flows out of your mouth. (This might take a little time, but if you are sincere, it will pay off more than any other effort.).

- **Do utilize your teeth as gates that prevent ugly speech "creatures" from getting out and gnawing on your spouse (or anyone else for that matter).** Worse than having poor communication skills is having the ability to clearly articulate your thoughts if all you want to do is say something mean or demeaning. Never say anything that will confuse or hurt anyone and start being good by practicing on your spouse. Think of mean speech as a verbal dagger aimed for the heart. There is never an acceptable reason for being mean.

It is ALWAYS the right time to say "I love you"

The rules are mathematical rules that work. Prove them yourself

Recognize the "Speech creatures" which are not limited to, but include:

criticism	sarcasm	insults
demanding	rudeness	impoliteness
inconsideration	shortness	snapping
"making fun of"	accusing	belittling
demeaning	ridiculing	being bossy
devaluing	frowning	complaining
nagging	silent treatments	mean looks
yelling	exploiting	comparing

Make note of your own habits rather than your spouse's. With trendy and misunderstood talk about standing up for yourself (at the expense of others), and comedies that promote cutting sarcasm as "funny," we are all swimming in the very dangerous waters of a cruel cultural environment (yes, look around at how "crude" has become acceptable). We need to be very careful not to behave like those who get a laugh at the expense of others. We must not imagine that the behavior we see all around us is fine for us, too. Remember, people who are teased do not think it is funny; they often feel humiliated even when they smile in order to fit in.

Your marriage is not a sitcom or TV series. Humorous moments that deteriorate into personal attacks under the guise of humor are devastating to sensitive people and hurtful to everyone else. Be quick to apologize (love is always being ready to say you are sorry) if you should inadvertently cross the line. Be quick to forgive if your spouse crosses the line. Breaking the habits of unkind speech should be a high priority as over-familiar behavior is at the root of this form of communication. Some people think it is okay to communicate with their spouses in ways that are not acceptable anywhere else. It is not okay, it's the opposite; treat your spouse as the most important person in the world. Still others think because they are not pointedly mean, they try to be "neutral". Not good enough. **Your role as a spouse calls for *overtly positive speech and behavior*.** Your spouse is the most important person in your life. Always speak lovingly to her or him. The responsibility is yours to protect your spouse from your stuff, as well as protect yourself from their stuff. Naturally, as you and your spouse adjust to this change and discover how deep the habits are, you may offend or be offended by an unintentional slip. The following analogy may help you get through the inevitable transition period, as you both work toward gaining control of your bad habits.

Imagine your child comes home one day and as he or she walks through the door, you notice signs of physical illness. You rush to cuddle your poor baby but before you can ask what's wrong, your precious vomits all over the place, including on your clothes; they couldn't help it! You could get mad, I suppose, but not for long as your main impulse is to care for them. Same way for your spouse who vomits unkindness; these traits are like a disease that must be eradicated by the carrier and seen as a disease by the puked upon; don't take it personally! Be understanding and get out of range. Don't puke back!

Control your mental behavior the same way you would control a dog. Don't let it "bite" or "bark"

Open your heart to your spouse and express your love at every opportunity. Don't start a conversation when you are angry. (Controlling the mind is an obligation for anyone who has one— would you let your dog bite someone?)

Try these "training wheels" to begin a conversation:

1. Internally say a quick little prayer for your spouse ("I pray that (spouse's name) feels Your Divine love and Grace . . ." (mean it!)

2. Silently recall a positive thought of your partner that will replace any adverse thought you may be subconsciously harboring, i.e., "I love seeing him or her smile . . ."

    The first two steps set the mind up properly.

3. Ask your spouse if it is a good time to talk, i.e., "Honey, is now a good time for you to chat a bit?"

    This is being proactively considerate.

Make these acts habits! Don't worry if your spouse is doing it or not; *you* do it.

Lessons For A Happy Marriage

If your conversation is getting tense you need to back up to the "I love you" part

Continue with these "training wheels":

1. Smile at your spouse. If you are too angry to smile, you need to compose yourself first.

   It is your face, and your spouse must look at it because you are asking for her or his attention, so . . .

2. Compliment your spouse, i.e., "You look so beautiful or handsome today. I'm glad you married me..."

   Giving a compliment to your spouse is like giving candy to a child; it is always appreciated.

3. Casually mention the topic of conversation, i.e., "I was thinking about how Junior is doing in school..."

4. Give your spouse a chance to express his or her views by pausing for a few seconds. If your spouse takes over the conversation, consider it a good thing and listen with interest to the views you are hearing. Remember you are in a discussion; you are not debating! Your goal is to share thoughts back and forth until you both feel aligned. No one should prevail. No one is right and no one is wrong. If your spouse wants you to go first, ask before you proceed, i.e., "Shall I start? . . . It seems that his grades are not where they should be. Do you see it that way too?" Men are typically more cerebral and women verbal, but whatever the dynamics of your own relationship are, it is fine. The emphasis is on consideration rather than fixed form. You will need to concentrate more on consideration and caring than on trying to be explicit. Being understood is far less important than being loving.

Be polite, considerate, and loving no matter how or what you are feeling, even if it means you have to stuff it. It is better to poison yourself than everyone around you. It is reckless and boorish to dump on another human being, and it is completely nuts to dump on the person whose love you want.

Don't take a hard position. No matter what, don't take a hard position. Just keep on talking until both of you are sharing the same perspective, or put the conversation off. It is far more important to be on the same page, even if it's the "wrong" page. Remember: harmony first. You are not running a war.

Do not allow errant thoughts and feelings to derail your relationship. Your relationship is your safety zone in life. It is perfectly okay to stop the conversation if it gets unfriendly. Just say, "I think I'm a little nuts. Can we talk about this later?"

Don't be gossipy. Communication is like pouring something into someone else's container. You have no right to pour toxic waste, especially to the one you have promised to protect, love, and serve.

If you are overwhelmed with negative emotion that is directed toward your spouse and you cannot get it under control, I suggest the following:

1. As you look your spouse in the eye, take their hand and passionately:

2. Say, "I love you and appreciate you."

3. Say, "I treasure your love."

4. Say, "If I seem out of sorts, I just want you to know your love is helping me and I'm sorry if you get any of my yucky stuff." (You may use a word other than *yucky* if you wish.)

> **Fools argue; wise men discuss**

Arguments are a total drag. Nothing is worthy of an argument. Creating or participating in an argument reflects your inability to understand your spouse's point of view. You are taking yours too seriously. Arguments begin when someone takes a stand or starts to blame the other (due to attachment or emotion). Arguments end only when one or both people surrender; that is not the right kind of surrender. If you win an argument, your spouse loses, and now you have beaten your spouse. That is the last thing you want.

There are much better ways to find solutions than arguing. An argument will create resentment and more arguments, not harmony. No matter what happens, refuse to argue. Don't allow yourself to get sucked in by your desire to prove your point. It is *never* worth it in a marriage. Can you recall a positive outcome from any argument? Have you ever won an argument that ended with a nice massage? If

> **Lawyers, politicians, and theologians routinely argue. It is fine for those who argue within a particular defined context; it is not fine for couples.**

you can't switch back to discussion, you must disengage. ("I need a breather; let's take a break.") Lawyers, politicians, and theologians routinely argue. It is fine for those who argue within a particular defined context; it is not fine for couples.

Discussions, on the other hand, are very cool. They breed new understanding and ideas that evolve into even better ideas. Begin without a preconceived attachment to what the outcome will be; a desire to find a solution *together* is the proper goal. Express your *ideas* to each other as ideas instead of conclusions. Enter discussions with a desire to get some good feedback, which will take your seed of an idea to the next level. Sometimes our first idea does not take into consideration enough options.

Example of conclusion talk: Sara watches too much TV.

Example of idea talk: Maybe Sara should watch less TV.

The purpose is to **avoid putting your spouse in the position of having to choose to go along with your solution or argue against it.** You might even say something like "There is a topic I would like to discuss."

Go into your conversation with an open mind so that you will generate more thoughts. Put aside conclusions you may have already reached on your own. Arguing different points of view will polarize you. (Very bad!) Listen to your partner's thoughts the same way you listen to your own; they are just ideas. When you frame your responses non-confrontationally, you open the door for more discussion without stepping on anyone's toes. Moreover, be patient. A discussion takes longer and gives you opportunities to praise your spouse until they are floating with your expressed love. When you decide on something together, you can be strong together so even if it is the two of you against the whole world, you will have each other's love and support. Remember, your spouse is on your side even when they forget it for a moment.

When either of you lose something, both of you suffer.

Example of a correct conversation: "Wow, did you see Johnny's report card? It would be hard to imagine he is feeling good about those grades. . . . I know what you mean. . . . Do you think he has been spending

> One of the most common misconceptions is thinking all problems need a solution right now. They can wait!

enough time doing his homework? . . . It must be *something*. . . . I agree with you. . . . What do you think would help him get better grades? . . . I can't be sure. . . . Maybe he is watching too much TV, what do you think? . . . Could be, that was a smart thought, I would feel better if he stayed home more nights, too."

Did you notice how you can't tell who is talking? That's how it's supposed to be. Both of you are on the same page right from the start and the page slowly takes the shape of your combined ideas. By the end of the conversation, you have both introduced possible reasons and solutions. Soon there is agreement, but no one took charge. No one has been rude or overbearing or anything other than a team player. Remember; unless there is alignment, there is no workable solution to any problem. There is a lot of power when you work together; there is a lot of pain when you work against each other.

One of the most common misconceptions is thinking all problems need a solution right now. They can wait! Most problems are only problems of perspective anyway. They only seem like problems. If you can't think of some input, it's okay to say so. If you can't handle more input, it's okay to say so. As a listener, open your mind to ideas you were not prepared to discuss. If you find your mind locking up on you, just say so in a nice way: "My mind is locking up, can we tackle this a bit later?" Then, Speaker, let it be. Say, "Okay, no problem. I'll just write down some notes so I don't lose my thoughts," thus acknowledging your partner's needs without crashing your enthusiasm.

- **Do not talk about things you hate.** Get rid of hatred as soon as you are aware of it coming to your mind. Hatred is poison; spit it into the toilet, not at your spouse!

- **Do not talk about little quirky things that your spouse does that bug you.** Do not overreact. If you have a tendency to be oversensitive, it is up to you to contain yourself during the conversation and work on your oversensitivity on your own. See quirky things your spouse does as cute. You can choose to complain and ruin everyone's day or compliment and uplift everyone's day—Be smart.

More Dos and Don'ts

Being "my self" should improve upon the status quo not degrade you

- **Do not talk about your sexual needs and what turns you on and off when you are about to have sex, are having sex, or you just had sex. Never present your needs and preferences as a negative.** Don't ever blame your spouse for not pleasing you because it will only make him or her nervous and less able to please you. When on a drive or walk talk about what would turn you on as if it is something you would like to try.

  Another method of kind communication in the area of sexual intimacy is to list your desires dispassionately and keep refining your list until all your anger and blame is gone. Then ask your spouse if she or he would like to see the list you made. (This is the default method). For some, it's fine to talk about sex as long as there is no expectation. The last lesson will open a completely new world to you; but don't peek!

"Real life" has come to mean low class and ignorant

- **Do not gossip.** Did I mention this before? Yes, I did! Gossip is like spreading weed seeds in your garden.

- **Do not *ever* raise your voice against those you love** (rules are different for kids). Vent your anger elsewhere; kick out thoughts of anger.

  Because raising one's voice is commonplace in many cultures, I will emphasize this point. All cultures have at least a couple of unbeneficial or destructive components; raising one's voice is one of them.

- **Do not speak in a demeaning or scolding voice;** remain as respectful as you would if you were speaking with the Pope or something.

Be your spouse's soul mate; it IS a choice. Let them see you as loving and supportive.

- **Do not correct your spouse.** It is not your place to correct him or her.

- **Do tell your spouse "I love you" as often as you can.** Feel the love before you say it. Don't say it mechanically. Once per hour is not too often, once a day is not enough.

- **Do compliment your spouse as often as you can.** Once per hour is not too often, once a day is not enough.

- **Do tell your spouse she or he is beautiful or handsome as often as you can.** Once per hour is not too often, once a day is not enough. There are two kinds of physical beauty. One is Hollywood beauty, which is beauty determined by proportionate and symmetrical features perfectly put together, as if the face you see was drawn by a commercial artist. This kind of beauty is easily recognizable and pleasing to the eye but does not tell anyone about the person contained within. You see real and true beauty through the eyes of your heart and soul. Your soul does not compare one person to another. Therefore, because of your marital closeness, you can see the goodness of your spouse manifested into his or her physical form as no one else can. Because of your special closeness, you have the unique ability to see that he or she is not just handsome or beautiful, but the most handsome or beautiful you have ever seen. By ignoring the few flaws they may have (or what you think of as flaws because of your Hollywood preferences), you will remember that you get to live with the most beautiful person in the world (just like you, of course).

- **Do tell your spouse you see them as the most beautiful or handsome.** Tell them often!

- **Do tell your spouse you appreciate them for their intelligence and beauty, as well as other positive qualities** (at least once a day).

- **Talk about your children.** The most important job you will ever have is to raise God's children for Him, and you need to take it very seriously so you don't come back as a cockroach. Okay, this may be an exaggeration—it's not like I know enough to have actually stated that—but obviously raising children is not something one should take lightly. We are not reptiles that lay eggs and walk off. You need to do all you can, and then some, to raise your children according to the highest principles you know. You and your spouse need to inspire each other to higher and higher child-rearing methods. Be creative with your love. Your efforts are never too great or wasted. Challenge yourself to be a better parent every day; take responsibility as a parent. Use your common sense as a guide—not trendy psychobabble or feel-good stuff that reduces your importance as your child's guide and authority.

- **Talk about your interests, work, and passions.**

- **Compliments are mandatory in a marriage because they add to the joy in your relationship.** Look for opportunities to throw out a surprise compliment, like, "Have I told you how beautiful you are?"

- **Receive compliments with both gratitude and humility.** Acknowledging a compliment is complimentary. Both speaker and listener need to look for moments to praise, even if it's just to say something like, "You are so cool. I am so happy I found you." Compliments are gifts and need to be acknowledged. Don't let compliments go to your head; let them go to your heart.

- **Talk about your good experiences.** Make it a point to express your appreciation for all the good in your life. Your life is too good to complain about, and you know it. Express gratitude as often as you can. You are safe in your relationship and may express your joy without being accused of false buoyancy.

- **Talk about your hard experiences and challenges.** Don't blame others or make your difficulties seem more than small items. If you see flaws all the time, you are defining yourself as overly critical. When you see goodness, you are defining yourself as a loving and grateful person. Challenges define your current curriculum (life is a school). Your partner will learn from your experiences—but your job as an emotionally challenged spouse is the same for every individual. Work through your emotional challenges individually. They were there before you met your spouse and remain until you conquer them.

The great temptation may be to "share the bad times," but that does not include an individual emotional challenge. It means you face life's challenges together providing love and support, not advice. I promise you it is better to respect boundaries in this case. Don't include your spouse in your mental trials. They cannot help you. If you think you are working on your personal trials together, you will not dig deeply to find your own inner strength, which is required to conquer them. When you are faced with tremendous trials, such as a marriage that is hurting, it is an ideal time to pray. God likes us to ask for help. For most of us, it's the only time we call.

There is a state called *crisis*. A crisis is always a matter of subjective perception. If it feels like a crisis you have allowed your mind to victimize you. Before you infect your relationship, do some calming exercises like deep breathing to get your emotions under control. It is fine to tell your spouse you are going through this process, but do not get into your issue. Merely say you are working through some "stuff" and apologize for seeming distant or preoccupied.

If your spouse asks for psychological advice give listening, love and support

- **Never offer advice when your partner discusses their challenges.** They are not asking for your help. They only want to share their struggles with you. Personal growth can come quickly, but it does not come by skipping steps.

Like constructing a building, one can lay the bricks of life quickly or slowly, but one cannot lay a brick atop thin air. The first layer of bricks must be there for one to lay the next. So it is with lessons of life; none can be skipped. We can barely see our own path, so it is unwise to think we can help another with guidance, no matter how convinced we may be that we see what is best for them. I have found this point to be vital to those who wish for love in their relationship to remain untainted.

Do not confuse your kids with your spouse or your spouse with your kids. Advising your spouse is taboo Advising your kids is vital.

We must allow people to progress at the pace they set for themselves, even when we can see by virtue of our outside perspective what appear to be the next logical steps. It is rude to offer our aid to anyone in the form of advice, even when asked for. You have no right to ask a person to change to fit your desire du jour. Share because there are thoughts and feelings you want to share, not fix. Be utterly respectful. This rule does not apply to our children. We are there for our kids. Our job is to teach them, by example and guidance, how to live in this world.

- **Talk about your moral and mundane worldly victories and defeats; sharing the lessons you have learned.**

- **Share your new ideas with enthusiasm.**

- **Talk about God.** God likes attention. God can do anything and have anything He wants at will, except for your love. Your love is God's, only when you give it. Share with each other your gratitude for His love and protection. Don't be shy about praying for your family.

- Lastly, and very importantly, **ask your spouse what she or he likes.** Are you a husband who buys his wife a blender for Christmas? Don't be a wife who makes her husband her favorite recipe assuming (or pretending) it's her husband's favorite, too. Don't ask him in a way that forces him to respond the way you want. If your best intentions and greatest efforts are not what satisfies your spouse, you are fooling yourself and burdening them with a quandary. Furthermore, it is not the job of your spouse to speak up if they do not like your gift. A gracious recipient always appreciates any gift given with the right attitude. Give gifts your spouse appreciates. Find out what they like by asking directly or indirectly. Make your spouse happy by discovering what makes them happy. Ask!

One time, I could not convince a very nice lady that she couldn't read her husband's mind; she was so convinced that she could! I finally had her husband write down his thoughts about a certain topic of my choice. Then I asked her to describe his position before I exposed his written ideas. She was way off! She was still fighting the obvious, even though I proved my point with our little experiment.

We like to think we are in tune or connected because it is romantic, but this ideal is less valuable to the relationship than just being nice. When you jump to conclusions about what your partner is going to say, you hurt them because you effectively derail or stifle their thought process. Because many people think *as they speak* and are not even sure what exactly they are going to say until it is all out, it is very rude to interrupt. Patiently listen with interest and adoration. The best rule is to never interrupt, nor interrupt someone who is interrupting you (take the high road).

When I am being interrupted, I like to think the person has to get it out before they forget what they have just thought of.

Sometimes the interrupter is nervous and doesn't even know they are interrupting; let it go. Magical relationships are simple. Be polite and considerate. True attunement is the act of giving love. If you continuously nurture the plant with loving care, the sweet fruit of marital bliss will come.

You may think your point of view is more valid and apropos than your spouse's, but it is not. Your correct spousal role is to be supportive of your spouse and never take a position contrary to theirs; it does no good to focus on areas of disagreement. If you have some contrary philosophical beliefs, i.e., views on the death penalty, keep it outside of your marital communication. It has no possibility of a positive impact on your marriage anyway and can only cause frustration if discussed with passion. (As you develop skills of diplomacy, you will be able to safely discuss volatile issues.) You do not have to agree on all of those things, but you do have to honor each other by appreciating that each of you came to your beliefs sincerely.

> **It is far better to be nice then to be "in tune". You can control being in tune.**

Concentrate on listening to the substance and feelings. Don't get distracted by either their or your emotions. Work through seeming differences by learning how to appreciate your spouse's reasoning; never criticize.

There are rare times when the challenge of supporting your spouse's positions is so very great. When that happens in your relationship, it is still your obligation to remain loyal and supportive while quietly speaking your views to your spouse (later); no one else should ever know you do not back your spouse's thinking or positions. Even our civil laws respect this ideal by not forcing a person to testify against their spouse; loyalty is not just about sexual fidelity. Don't hold your reality so tightly that you are not able to appreciate the point of view of your true love. Stop your mind from taking things too seriously. Remember, *how you treat each other will make a difference*, **not your views on various topics**. Keep your peace by knowing you are doing your best. Never argue later about topics or behavior.

Everyone has his or her own style and level of communicating and that is completely fine; you don't have to be perfect, you just have to

> **Excuse and ignore any display of anger, stubbornness, narrow-mindedness, etc.**

try. Remember to never work on other people's style, just your own. Respect your spouse's individuality as you would have your spouse respect yours.

Practice attentive listening religiously

When you can hear other people's ideas without feeling internal resentment or criticism, you will know you are being an objective listener; you have discovered the most important tool of communication. Become a good listener! Being a good listener means being empathetic (caring) while dispassionate (not overly identified).

Try the following technique: Place an imaginary table between you and the person with whom you are speaking. As the person speaks, let her or his points collect on the table like so many objects. Categorize and prioritize them. *Do not react to anything.* On this imaginary table, separate the thoughts that are offensive from the thoughts you believe require discussion. Take your sweet time and examine the points of communication that you resonate with, with an eye toward really understanding what the points mean to the person, and what you may contribute in a positive way (saying you don't like an idea is not positive). Ask the speaker about your favored points: "I think what I hear you saying is such and such. Did I get it right?" Respond to the points that require discussion by saying something like, "I think I understand what you mean; that's pretty cool. I never looked at it that way." (Throwing in a compliment is always wise.)

You will soon feel calm because you will not be a victim of too complex a conversation. You will have chosen your topics. What you left on the table was probably not that important anyway. If your spouse wants a response to the topics you missed, apologize and ask if it is okay for you to think about them. If it is a "burning" issue (you need a new car and today is the only day to get one—you must choose even if it's a bad choice), you are obligated to do your best. You can first say you need more understanding. It does not mean you have to come to conclusions. You should at least try to take the edge off the issue with your spouse. Remain patient!

Your partner should calm down (if not, excuse yourself until peace is restored—but not to show how cool you are). No matter what you do, don't jump into a fight, no matter how inflammatory a comment seems. It is unlikely the comment was meant to be cutting. If it actually was meant to be mean, it was merely your spouse's momentary inability to cope that allowed the comment past their ivory gates (teeth), reflecting a weakness in them, not a flaw in you.

People express themselves primarily for their own sake; they want recognition, respect, appreciation, and so forth. Be different; speak to give recognition, respect, appreciation, and so forth. Do not criticize any point made by anyone, because when you do, you attack him or her personally. Just work toward understanding and creating discussion.

Remember, good communication does not translate into getting others to fulfill your desires. If that is the measure you use, the correct term would be good salesman or manipulator. Good communicators are not necessarily good negotiators, nor does your marriage require good negotiating skill. Save those skills for when you buy your next car! A good communicator is user-friendly.

Make your partner feel good whenever you communicate with them. We are all simple people with the need to interact in a way that makes our partners feel good. *Always* send your communications on the vehicle of loving feelings no matter what you are saying. Some smart people repeat in their minds, "I love you honey" or "I am so lucky" while they are speaking with their spouse. Others think only about how to sweeten their communication even more. Use any method that works for you. You should love each other even when one or both of you feel lower emotional states that are temporarily on central stage. Do not allow any nasty thoughts to block loving feelings.

Listening, really listening, with interest is an important tool. Think back to when you were courting. When you listen and understand your spouse's point of view, you will be surprised at how sweet it is to see through their eyes. You will see in ways you never thought of. You can bridge great gaps in perspective with appreciation and sincere adoration. There is so much to appreciate, but we fall into the easy habit of just seeing flaws. Ugly thoughts crowd out the right thoughts of appreciation and admiration. Kick ugly thoughts out of your mind!

Control your mind. Don't let your mind wander when your spouse is speaking, and don't let errant opinionated thoughts interrupt your listening. Behave. Imagine you are speaking to the

You have great power in speech. Use it to please your spouse

Your spouse is the most important person in your life

Dalai Lama or something. Be really nice and just smile with your lips closed if you have to until you have controlled your thoughts.

Maintain thoughts of love at all times. No matter what is spoken, the feeling of love needs to be there; tuning into "love" is worth the effort. Communicate lovingly and smile to your spouse. I have met with so many couples who had not smiled at each other for so long they forgot how. I forced them! I had them hold each other's hands, look into each other's eyes, smile, and say something like:

"Honey, I married you forever and have forgotten my vows to be loving and loyal. I am sorry. I have taken you for granted. I have not adored you. I have been demanding and selfish. I have judged you and expected you to make me happy when I faltered. I know it is not your job to make me happy. It is my greatest pleasure to do all I can to be there for you as your best friend and the greatest lover the world has ever known. You are precious to me. I have not treated you well; and though I can never repair the past, I can change the future. I will. You are the one I chose to adore and honor. You are the one I wish to remain with for the rest of my life. I love you and will do all I can to demonstrate my feelings of love..." Try this!

I urge you to use the above words or write your own. Then have a renewal moment with your spouse. Love will always transcend any momentary negative feelings and thoughts. So you must hold on to the love and do your best to protect your relationship from degenerate thought habits.. Nobody is perfect, so patiently and lovingly allow for slips.

Humility is never humiliating

When you find yourself in a hole, the first thing to do is stop digging! Here's how...

Saying "I'm sorry" is a way for you to communicate a truce AND stop the mind from compounding the problem with excuses and other forms of defensiveness. It's a clearing method that does not necessarily have to mean you want forgiveness or you did something you are sorry for. "I'm sorry" means there is a misunderstanding and you need to start from a few steps back. Say, "I'm sorry" the moment tensions begin to define the conversation; better too early than too late (though it is never too late). The first one to say, "I'm sorry" gets a prize. This tool is amazing! It works so well in so many situations that you should use it (sincerely, of course) even when you are not sure it is appropriate.

As soon as your spouse "attacks," you say, "I'm sorry!" Try it, say it out loud. It is meant to defuse situations not people. It sends a loud and clear signal that you would rather be wrong than get into an altercation. When used with "I love you," it is all-powerful. Does that mean it disarms your spouse? Maybe, sometimes, but what it really does is it takes the user out of the frame of mind that prolongs disputes. If one person is throwing mudballs and the other is throwing kisses, there is not much chance of escalation. Soon things will calm down and (sometimes after a period of disengagement) you will be able to resume your discussion.

Please adopt the above technique; it works!

People need to feel connected and understood. One of the big reasons to get married is to feel part of a family. It is natural and intuitive to communicate pleasantly with those you love, but our culture promotes some gnarly practices that undermine relationships. Venting is an example of misguided thinking. About venting, I can tell you venting is always a bad thing to do. All venting does is distract you from solving your problems, whether attitude, perspective, or whatever. One therapist told my wife and me to take turns actively listening to each other's grievances; boy was that stupid! If you have a grievance, it means you are blaming someone else for your pain. That is like walking into a tree and getting mad at the tree for stepping in front of you. Eliminate venting as an option. The only exception is you may complain to God . . . all you want ☺. Often there is confusion about *what* should or should not be communicated. The current idea of being open and freely expressing one's self has become absurd. Most people think they need to blurt out whatever is on their mind in the name of "honesty" and in order to feel that they are being "open."

Truthful does not mean hurtful. Expressing temporary feelings that cause others pain is rude. Telling your spouse you had a premarital relationship with his or her best friend, for instance, in order to "clear the air," will only create future fear and immediate pain. Or finally releasing things you chose to "bottle up" (even if it was so you wouldn't hurt anyone) because you finally can't hold it

Venting Is Bad

Venting is always a bad idea. But if you must complain God is a good listener and you won't hurt God's feelings.

anymore is not a successful strategy either. If you need to unburden your mind, it is a great idea to eliminate the bad habits that got you into trouble in the first place; those habits are the burden. Guilt and shame are useless demons that do not go away when you share your flaws. Your spouse can do nothing to help you in this area. You need to make every effort to keep your relationship a sacred space, not a dumping ground. Do not deliver guilt and shame, only love and support. Take control over which thoughts and feelings you wish to entertain, especially when it is difficult.

The topic of what you should and should not hold back from telling your spouse can be vast and is too complex to be covered adequately in these lessons. I am not advocating maintaining a secret life outside of your marriage. I just caution you to use common sense and discrimination. It is not beneficial to bear all. In most scenarios, you will only create unnecessary drama and bad feelings.

Someone I know suspected his wife of having extramarital sex. When he asked a person he respected what he should do, he was told he should wear a condom when he had sex with his wife and try to improve his relationship. This was neither a joke nor a flip answer. It was the wisest of all answers because it is real. Look at the alternatives; no matter what you come up with when you play out the possibilities, they are all bad. He received the best possible advice to refocus his attention on being a great husband and win his wife back. Meanwhile, he was protecting himself from the real or imagined threat to his physical health.

Demonstration of Good communication

"Hi honey."

"Hi."

"Sweetie, I have something I'd like to talk about. Is now a good time for you?"

"Okay, thanks for asking. That was really considerate."

"Well, I just want to be sure."

"Awww!"

"Honey, in case it comes out like complaining, I just want to let you know that these are my feelings and I'm not asking you to change anything. I love you so much. I only feel fortunate that we are together."

"I understand, and that was sweet of you to say. I feel the same way."

"Well, you know how sometimes you are in such a hurry that you may forget to close a drawer? I'm not complaining about it, but I don't want you to think it's you if I seemed irritable today. I'm working on detaching from it because I know it's not such a big deal, but I don't want you to feel put off if I seem to be in a mood. I love you so much and don't want to hurt your feelings."

"Wow, I had no idea that you were so impacted. I know you aren't asking me to change or work on this, but if it will help I sure want you to be happy. I'm sorry I left the drawer open. Can I massage your shoulders? Would you like that now?"

"You are so sweet. No thank you. I just wanted to be sure you are okay."

The above conversation may seem like too much, like an exaggeration to make a point, but it isn't. When you take vitamins, you take the whole dose. When you eat, you eat a full meal. When you communicate, you need to do the whole deal.

This format does not apply to emergencies, like warning about an oncoming car.

Always see your spouse in the kindest light; <u>just as you want them to see you.</u> When it comes to filtering this way, it is not blind ignorance—it is, in a word, loyalty.

Some say you should choose your battles—heck with that! **Choose not to battle at all!** Valuing philosophical points of view above marital bliss is not cool. So much goes into how we come to our various points of view and even the most important topics are often clouded by our inability to communicate our heart's feelings accurately.

Take responsibility (the word *responsibility* is extreme but defines where the effort needs to be made) for properly communicating what you want to say. If it was complex, be sure you were clear in your communication by asking what they heard you say. Remember, you are not checking on *them*. If they did not understand you, it is because you didn't speak their language and you need to correct yourself. You should be as clear as possible; listening spouse, be patient! **If your point(s) were not understood, take responsibility** by saying something along the lines of, "I didn't do a great job of expressing myself, . . ." then ask permission to try again. "May I try again?" It may be wise to play out your communication in your own head first to hear how it sounds. Ask

Primitive practices, like stoning harlots, eventually lose their social acceptance. Complaining is primitive and will eventually lose acceptance. Be one of the first to consider it unacceptable.

Use words and gestures that reflect love and support

yourself if you would understand your own points. "Honey, would you mind telling me what you heard? I just want to be sure I said what I meant to say" or "Oh, I can see how you got that but it's not what I meant. May I try again?"

Be humble. It is so easy to sound like a drill sergeant screaming at the recruit, "Did you hear me, Dirtbag!" Listening spouse, it takes some practice, so cut some slack. Sympathize with your partner's weakness in this area. In your mind, see the effort and not the flaws; soon you will both be speaking the same language.

When your spouse is talking, it is about your spouse; and it is not respectful to shift the conversation to your own needs and ideas. This, of course, comes back to common courtesy and not being over-familiar. If you feel like engaging, you must do whatever it takes to get in the mode of a best friend who sympathizes and offers support without commentary or advice. You are the spouse, not the priest or some dictator or any other advisor. Obviously, this rule does not include the husband who has worked on cars all his life not being asked for his suggestions about a car purchase; or the wife not being asked what kind of fragrance to use in the bathroom. Common sense still supersedes any rule, unless the speaker has invoked the rule that no advice is wanted. As a listener, you are not a "fixer." Remember, you cannot change anyone, so be a great listener. Allow the speaker to get it *all* out without interruption or questions.

Smile, touch lightly, laugh, wink, be cute, and turn each other on the way you did when you first met. One wife complained she couldn't get her hubby to clean the garage and asked me what to do. My suggestion was to use her feminine charms instead of flailing arms. This doctrine is an inspiration for common sense and creativity. Whatever you guys come up with is cool as long as you are kind and considerate. Spouses don't work for each other. They serve each other lovingly and gladly because they want to. The "want to" can come from within or can be stimulated with sweet bribes. *Enjoy* your marriage!

Be patient with yourself and each other. Just making some effort to gain proficiency as a communicator will bring grand and noticeable results much faster than you can imagine. You will become more aware of yourself and others. You will feel more in control of yourself.

A communicator is expressing what is inside his or her mind at a particular moment, and may have little, or nothing, to do with you. Do not take it personally. At best, you may be a catalyst and/or sounding board; do not take it personally! At worst, you are a convenient dumping ground; do not take it personally!

We wrongly imagine that when our spouses scold us it is because we have done something wrong or we have been misunderstood; neither is likely to be true. What they say may work on you, eat at you, haunt you, make your stomach turn and drive you crazy, **until you learn to accept other people's communications impersonally. Now that you know this, be there for your spouse!**

Sometimes your spouse may come up with some crazy intense communication. Maybe you will be called a liar, or a cheat, or a nag, or another similar insensitive, in-your-face comment. No matter how inappropriate it is, remember it is not about you unless you make it so; let it go! If you can't let it go right away, you need to disengage before you say something equally insensitive.

I must draw the line somewhere. If I keep going with communication, this lesson will turn into a book all on its own. I'm sure others have written comprehensive studies for those who desire to learn more. There is more than enough here for those who want a happy marriage.

Do not take it personally

Communication is very powerful. Use it to express love, support and adoration.

Lessons For A Happy Marriage

Exercises for Communication

The more loving actions you put into your communication, the more joyous your marriage will be. I have seen normal people learn just a few of the above rules for communication and change their marriage forever. I bumped into a client years after we had met who told me that even though they were still having financial problems, their marriage was the sweetest part of their lives. (When we met professionally, they were giving it one last shot. We met a total of two and one-half hours). Even though you know enough at this point to have a successful and happy marriage, keep reading. The best is yet to come.

1. Always pay attention to the results of your communications. The simpler (less topics) your communication the easier it will be to tie a reaction to what you say.

2. Assign times to say short and sweet tidbits. Make "I love you" one of them. Never stop.

3. Write a list of honest praises and commit yourself to expressing them.

4. Commit yourself to hearing abusive communications such as criticism and complaints as a weakness on the part of your spouse. Train yourself to feel compassion instead of resentment

5. Always remember that you hold the keys to happiness. One key is your communication.

Business Arrangement Mentality

"What if I do my part and my spouse doesn't?" is the most deadly and difficult attitude to overcome. If *you* are asking this question, you will hold back your efforts. If you think your *spouse* is asking this question, you will hold back your efforts. One man, after I told him he needed to make the effort even though he thought his wife was cheating on him, asked me if I expected him to be a saint. My reply was that becoming a saint was a risk I thought he could live with, but holding back his effort until he was convinced his wife would match his was a guaranteed slide into divorce court.

This attitude defines an "us-and-them" or business relationship, not a marriage. Because neither person *completely* trusts each other (which is natural and something that is part of our human nature), we must not expect unconditional trust from our spouse; at the same time you still must try to do all you can to be trusting and trustworthy.

There is an unwritten universal assumption that both of you will contribute the same amount of energy toward making your relationship successful; it seems only fair. However, it is impossible for two people to meet at the proverbial halfway point; thus the conundrum! Behaving well will transcend this nastiness. Making your behavior dependent on your own ideas of how to behave rather than how you are treated will save you.

There is a story about a king who sent his most trusted warrior into a dark cavern to beat out the darkness with his club. What the warrior could not do in a million trillion years, a child was able to accomplish instantly; with a match! Using the right tool is the key to success. The wrong tool will not work no matter how determined

Fairness means "sides." There are no sides in marriage.

you may be. You should be starting to see that all you have to do is behave in a reasonable way because it is better for you as an individual. You, too, will destroy the darkness with direct methods that require only normal behaviors.

Desire for fairness comes from insecurity and selfishness.

Why do we have the desire for fairness? Some of you are thinking, "So, what's wrong with that? What's wrong with fairness?" I can't tell you how many times I have heard, "I just want it to be fair." Little do you realize; Desire for fairness comes from insecurity and selfishness and never can be satisfied! I'm not a Sunday School teacher "trying to show ya da way ta redemption!" Instead I will prove to you—strike that!—I will show you how to prove to yourself that the way to get what you want, and more, is to shift your thinking to "correct" thinking, the thinking that brings lasting results by *working in harmony with human nature.* There is never such a thing as fair. Someone who has a particular point of view—filled with all sorts of fears, biases, and prejudice—always weighs fairness in the abstract. How do you weigh good and bad deeds, anyway?

The truth is there is no such thing as fair from a truly objective point of view, and the desire for fairness will drive you nuts. Of all the killers of a loving relationship, this is by far the most "crazy making." Once the fear of unfairness takes hold, it develops a veritable army of fear-based reasons to maintain a scrutinous eye on every word, thought, and deed that will support the seeming negative. The way to avoid this trap of the mind is to reverse the spotlight of critical attention.

When you put goodness into your relationship without expecting anything in return, you will achieve happiness no matter how your partner behaves

Correct your own behavior, and instead be inwardly appreciative and complimentary of your partner's unique behaviors. When you put goodness into your relationship without expecting anything in return, you will achieve happiness no matter how your partner behaves. Your mind may always tell you it isn't fair, or that you are sad. Reject such thoughts as quickly as they enter your mind. Lasting peace and happiness do not come as the result of external conditions. Break the chains of suffering driven by the fear that you are not getting what you deserve. Stop your mind from overemphasizing the illusionary lack; instead be appreciative of all you have. Give to your relationship without expectation of a return. When you feel taken advantage of or taken for granted, instead of defending your space, offer more of yourself. The mind is like a little child who cannot be satisfied for long and gets in the habit of complaining and wanting more. Don't let it ruin your day with justifications for its petulance.

Discipline your mind to be happy as a giver. Fear is the enemy, isn't it? The mind tells you that if you change and your spouse remains the same you will be taken advantage of and that would be the end of it. Instead of wanting to please your spouse without thinking, "what's in it for me," you have given in to the fear of coming up short in the bargain. Is this how you are? If not, please accept my apology for being so strong. But for those who need to hear it, I have been far too gentle. If you believe this now, please understand that the perspective you currently hold is evidently not working, so go along with me as the ideas unfold. It will *all* make sense, and it all works. If you are committed to rescuing the most important relationship you will ever have and are not willing to settle for a mediocre marriage, the wisdom in this book will take you there. If you have the attitude of "nothing but complete success will do," then you will succeed. Never give up! You can do it!

You must never have expectations of anyone but yourself. I know this is a radical concept in today's world and our materialistic culture, but I will demonstrate the veracity of this concept in practical and logical ways. The people who resist this principle the most are the ones who need to study it the most. If your mind is intensely resistant and coming up with all sorts of exceptions, it means your life and happiness are controlled by everything and everyone but you.

Please change your attitude from "What's in it for me?" to "What can I do for my lover?"

When Mother Theresa said "Give until it hurts" she was being a bit sneaky. She knew that giving only brings happiness. The hurt she describes is selfishness (in its many forms) trying to deceive you and twist you away from joy producing behavior. Do what you know you should do, not what you "want" to do. Then you will find happiness.

Never give up! You can do it!

Recap

You have learned what the three killers of relationships are and how to combat them and keep them out of your own marriage.

The following lessons will convey the foundational principles of marriage. You will learn about what drives you and your spouse. It will all seem so basic, as truth always is, and your own understanding will bring you great relief as well as golden opportunities for a joy filled marriage.

Reaffirmation

*T*ake a major step in the right direction. Read this lesson through at least once before commencing with the techniques.

Make a deep and sincere effort to ignore all past bad feelings and thoughts; step out of the jungle of despair and feel the cool sunny clearing of marital love and joy. Put aside all challenging topics and hurts with the intention of putting them out of your relationship altogether. You do not need an agreement to do this; only *your* efforts matter.

Sit close enough to hold each other's hands, face each other, look into each other's eyes and hold each other's gaze.

As you look in your spouse's eyes, without saying anything, recall the most pleasant thoughts about your spouse and see her or him as you did when you were standing at the altar ; recall those feelings and thoughts.

See your spouse through the eyes of love and admiration. Your spouse has flaws as do you. Ignore the flaws; push negation from your mind. Remain internally positive.

Now, internally, say a purely supportive prayer for your spouse, such as, "I pray my love feels love as deserved and has so much joy they seem drunk with it. . . ." Pray for those things you would wish for yourself and really mean it. Seek nothing in return. Assume the virtue of a selfless saint. Do not pray for your spouse to change or understand you.

Now, in turn.

Slowly, with deep love and great sincerity, say, "Honey," (or any term of endearment your spouse likes) "I love you and now realize I have not been treating you with the love and respect I showed you before we were married. I'm sorry.

I supplied this technique as an excuse for you to break the ice and start experimenting with positive behaviors-take advantage of it!

Take turns.

(Pause)

"I can now see how that hurts you and I am truly sorry.

(Pause)

"I love you and want you to be happy.

(Pause)

"I love you and really want to be married to you.

(Pause)

"From this moment I will do my best to break my bad habits of not honoring you. . . . I will make a conscious and continuous effort to break the habit of treating you poorly. . . . **I will redevelop the good habit of treating you the way I really want to**,

"With love,

"With respect, with appreciation

(Pause)

"I will treat you as my greatest treasure—because you are! You are my best friend."

You respond as follows:

"Thank you for expressing such loving thoughts.

"I needed to hear it, and it fills my heart with love I have always had for you.

"I feel the same way.

"Honey, I love you too; and though I have created many filters and walls through fear, I think I feel your love.

"I will focus on that love because I desire your love and devotion so much.

"I too, will break my habits of mistreating you.

"I am so sorry we have been hurting each other; with all my might I will break the habits of hurting you.

"I love you and want to be here for you.

Eyes are the window to the soul. Look into your spouse's eyes with deep love and appreciation.

"I want you to be happy; I want you to look forward to talking to me and spending time with me. I will bring back the lover I took away from you so that you will want to be with me more than anything or anyone else.

"I will also treat you as my greatest treasure because you are; you are my best friend."

Do not allow doubts to ruin this moment. You both want the same thing and need to protect your mind from habits of failure, doubt, and the satanic suggestion that your spouse doesn't mean it as much as you do.

When uttered with sincerity (remember you are in control of your own mind), the words in this lesson will reopen doors that have shut out your great love.

Most couples are initially afraid to open up again. They imagine it is important to first settle the current issues of disagreement before they open up again. That's just plain stupid and upside down. It is so much easier to settle real disagreements from a place of goodwill. End the war right now; at least your side of it. Stop suffering. Be nice. Be trusting. Be a loving spouse. If for some bizarre reason your spouse doesn't respond with love, that's her or his problem. You must behave rightly even when you think the situation calls for you to be resentful or 'in control.'

The above is not meant to create a temporary period of peace, guys. This is it. This is the beginning of your life of harmony. It's completely up to you. Don't let habits that brought you down creep back in. Insist on feelings of joy and love. They are your birthright and normal condition. If they go away, it's because you chased them away. You are the master of your destiny. It is all up to you. I'm just reminding you, right? This is all so simple and obvious, yet breaking habits is not so easy. It is way easier, though, than the alternative. End the self-inflicted suffering right now.

The effort to make your marriage blissful is much less then the suffering that comes from not making the effort

Points I wish to remember

Anatomy of a Marriage

We are mortal... until we express love; then we are Divine.

*I*f you walk to the edge of a ten-foot cliff, you stop because you know about gravity without thinking about it. No one needs to memorize, "I will stop when I get to the edge of a cliff." The preceding lessons describe what people do wrong, but knowing the killers is not enough to ensure a joyful marriage. You need to know how everything ties together so your actions and thoughts are as automatic as driving a car. Understand the construction of marriage so that you know what to do through applied common sense.

There are tons of books and even entire talk shows dedicated to the subject of marital relationships without describing what marriage actually is. The psychologists (who are one of the few "legal" vendors of marital advice despite their ineffectiveness) produce new and improved studies as often as detergent companies produce new and improved dish soap. (I heard on a PBS program that less than 10 percent of psychologists' clients find success!) However, once you understand marriage, joy is inevitable. You just need to know! Then instead of feeling helpless, needy, compelled, or trapped in a co-dependent relationship (not knowing what the heck you did this time), you will feel growing love and synergy. You will see for yourself and recognize the unrestrictive nature of a properly functioning relationship as well as all the soft spots in your own behavior that require a little special attention. By looking at the inner workings, you will be able to take control over your own behavior without confusion or other negative feelings because you will see how it all fits together. It is unthinkable to pour water into your car's gas tank because you know that will wreck it. By knowing how your marriage works, you will graphically understand what behaviors you do not want to pour into your marriage and those you do. It is less complicated than you may think.

The following illustration defines what you signed up for when you got married, not a poet's starry-eyed vision nor a cynic's depressing view—this is the real thing! The definition of marriage is simplicity itself (like gravity).

You and your spouse were (and will always remain) individuals. Here you are; the two of you, oblivious to each other's existence.

You and your spouse were and will always remain individuals

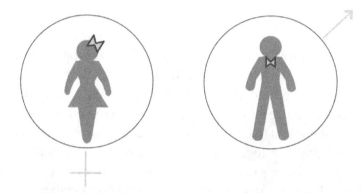

Then, at some magical moment, you met each other. It might have been a look, a smile from across the room at a party, an e-mail on an internet site, it doesn't matter. At the moment of first mutual contact your relationship began as a brand new entity. A spark appeared that grew into a living creation, created by the two of you and available to only the two of you. It may be defined as a unique, separate space made only from that which you and your spouse contributed.

What you put into the sacred space of your marriage relationship defines it.

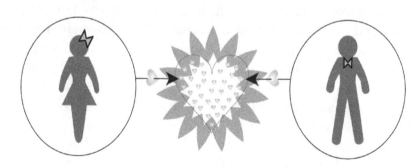

The space is accessible to only the two of you and what is in it is what you put in it. Your actual relationship is something "outside" of you both.

This container became your Sacred Space in which only the two of you share your love and a great deal of your lives.

Your first contact, illustrated by arrows coming from each of the smaller hearts with a little heart attached to it represents sweet input—a smile or kind word, some kind, and loving expression. These were decidedly positive inputs. If that first, sweet contact were the only contact you ever had and you never, ever saw each other again, the relationship would remain etched in your mind as a positive relationship forever. If you never, ever saw each other again, you would go to your grave with a positive feeling toward each other. This is logical to you, right? Let's continue down that pathway of thinking.

You keep adding only positives (hearts) into your relationship and your relationship grows and remains only positive, right? Each kind gesture and word positively contributes to the relationship, giving it depth and history.

Your relationship is the sum total of what you put in it: the good, bad, beautiful, and ugly. If all you ever put into your relationship is sweetness, respect, and positive expressions, that is all that will ever be in your relationship space, period! Get it? If you only put sugar in a glass of water, it will be sweet. The more sugar, the sweeter it is. Your marriage is the same. It is the space you and your spouse go into and put "stuff" into. Only the two of you have access to your marital space.

As time goes on after your first meeting, you keep adding kindness, (hearts) to your relationship space, and things just keep getting better. Both of you think of the other, "this one is a keeper," as your sacred space keeps filling with sweet little hearts. You learn

Your marriage is comprised of only that which you put into it. Fill your marriage with sweetness

more about one another; it is kind and loving input that creates the relationship you both want to be in. Both of you contribute to building this expanding relationship, this sacred space; you enjoy the space you are building together; you both cherish your relationship. It is all rather beautiful, isn't it?

Then you blow it! After some time, one of you "slips" and says or does something mean. One of you gets comfortable enough to allow a bad thought or feeling to take hold in your mind and you "test" the relationship by saying something mean or you behave in a way that is not beneficial for your true love. It could be almost anything—a terse response, a critical comment, an effort to control or any one of countless possibilities. Instead of putting in a heart, you threw a "mudball."

What happens next is possibly the beginning of the end of an otherwise joyous marriage. As soon as the mudball is perceived by the receiving target, they bring in walls and filters that are needed in the "world." These walls and filters are essential for existing without being destroyed by terrors we must confront every day. Each of us has developed walls and filters that work for us. They are not supposed to be used or needed in our marriage, our sacred space... But, we are not supposed to be attacked either!

You stepped onto the proverbial slippery slope when you were not consciously kind. You probably can't recall the first slip when one of you said something callous or behaved inconsiderately, but obviously it happened. It had to have happened, right? There had to be a first time! (And please don't hit me with, "we're only human," or "everybody argues." Why should you accept such limitations? Mistakes excused are mistakes that will multiply.) Before the first mudball, your relationship was filled with hearts.

Visualize a mudball being thrown by one of you toward the other. It is not a pretty sight! Neither one of you would literally bend over and scoop up a handful of mud, fashion it into a mudball, then hurl it at the other in anger or because you had a bad day. A physical mudball being thrown by either of you is grotesque and likely unimaginable. Yet the metaphorical mudball is no less painful! Why were you so mean?

Both of you launched a mud ball into the sacred space. The first mud ball went pretty much unnoticed. It flew in from one of you and because it was unexpected, the other did not recognize it

Before the first mudball, your relationship was filled with sweetness

as a mudball; so it pretty much went flying out the other side of the space. It is important to visualize this because the point is when a mudball goes unnoticed or uncaught, it can't damage anything (negative thoughts are mudballs, too).

The dynamics are like this: The first offender felt it was okay because there were no protests, no "don't ever do that again" reactions (they were not even sure if what they perceived was *real*). The perpetrator was then emboldened to sling another. After all, it felt good to vent (and the psych community says it is good for us) and there was no obvious cost. (Venting was actually encouraged by the Western psychological community in general until the mid-nineties. It is very destructive to both the venter and ventee). Then comes the response once they "get" what just happened. The reaction is "they slapped me, so it must be okay to do it back." Then BOOM! We now have one good slap bringing on another. The mudballs are flying. And what do we do when someone takes a shot at us? Correct.

We put up our walls and filters; AND move up our offensive artillery just in case we feel like hurling our own insults. I know some of you become victims and don't overtly retaliate. But all who get nailed manage to retaliate in some fashion. We don't want or need mudballs, walls, or filters in our sacred space. We need loving support, sweetness, compassion and understanding. However, once the attacks begin, it gets even worse than the rest of the world in the once sacred space. We are compelled to erect our worldly defenses. We try to make our walls impenetrable barriers. We deny access to attacks we perceive as potentially lethal. We also end up blocking out the hearts of marriage building positive communications. The downward spiral begins and continues until intentionally halted.

Filters are our way of seeing things based on our individual understanding of life's hazards. No one is able to judge the importance of our individual filters. We filter so that we can

Walls and Filters are essential to survival in the world-but not in your marriage.

Walls create barriers of privacy.

Filters are lenses that allow you to see through false pretenses.

Your love never goes away; it just gets smothered by the mud of indifference and hostile behavior

function in the world without opening ourselves up emotionally to potential heartaches. There is so much pain in the world it would kill us to take it all in. **Marriage is meant to be your "safety zone."**

When you bring your walls and filters into your sacred space, you lose the ability to taste the sweetness you built together. Love never went away. It just got covered underneath layers of mud. Walls and filters keep out danger, but they also block important feelings you need to share with your spouse. One of the biggies you wanted in your marriage was a trusted and trusting confidant, a best friend. The walls and filters we rely on in our day-to-day dealings are harmful to marital relationships and counter what we are trying to achieve in terms of trust and feelings of security. I do not condemn those who retain some of the walls and filters; I just encourage a relaxation of your dependence on them over time. I also advocate a mutual understanding that if the walls and filters seem hostile, they are not intended to be aggressive; they are defensive! The sacred space of marriage is a place you do not bring your walls and filters. You don't need them in your sacred space, but they came in on what became "sides" within your space. They are now covered with mud. I always illustrate the mud covering the sacred space with brown scribbles covering up the pretty pink hearts; not a heartwarming image. Folks became very emotional when they saw the graphic illustration of what they had done to their relationship. It isn't too late; clear it out. Lose the mud!

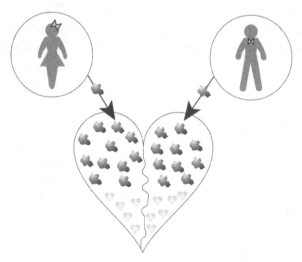

What do you do now? Your sacred space is filled to the bursting point with muddy walls, and you can barely feel each other's love. You don't trust each other or yourselves.

Love is super powerful and enduring, but mud has buried your love. The love is still there, you can feel it, but it seems dwarfed by the hurt. I say your love is a giant sun eclipsed by a small smudge on the window of your mind. So wipe away the smudges of wrong thoughts and enjoy your great love. I know how you feel. It is so overwhelming! Nevertheless, what can now take place for you is cool because it works for everyone without exception.

It's natural to believe your trust has been betrayed. Many people believe that is a big reason for divorce. "How can I ever trust my spouse again?" But you must remember that you have also betrayed the trust of your spouse. It makes no difference who is the bigger jerk. There is no way of measuring jerkiness or figuring out who went first. Both of you behaved inappropriately.

Both of you share something in your relationship that is hard to argue against. You share the incentive to start fresh with each other and observe the rules that bring success. If you have children, you have a billion times the incentive of those who do not, but even those who do not have children need not fail.

Most of the current despair, pain, and confusion you are currently burdened with will be almost completely gone in less than two weeks from the time you make up your minds that this is worthy of your efforts. By reminding yourself (never each other) that you are responsible for the mess, and only because you didn't know any better (self-blame is not cool either), you can forgive your spouse and move forward. The greater the effort to be sweet, the faster the mind shifts. I have seen couples leave gnarly pasts behind quickly. It makes no sense to want to go back and relive the pain of past mistakes. That would be like putting the flat tire back on the car. So here is what you can do:

Have you ever made soup from scratch? Sometimes we might taste it in the process and discover too much of something that makes the soup yucko (beyond adjusting). Have you tried to take out that ingredient? It is impossible. When the soup is bad, there is only one thing left to do; dump it out. How that translates in this case is that we dump all of our hurt feelings, anger, resentment, fears, walls and mudballs—everything that does not belong.

Behaving lovingly from now on is the shortcut to a happy marriage. Most effects are immediate.

What's left is the basic infrastructure of commitment: love, loyalty, and vision of future joy—the tangibles. Let the bad stuff go and refuse to let the mind reinstall all the fear and pain; just refuse to allow negative thoughts to come in or take root. Though this is the hardest part, it will work because I will give you techniques and you have everything to gain by making the effort.

The foundation of love is very strong. It's the mud covering the golden love that must be removed and not reintroduced. If mud manages to come in again, just dump it again and refocus on putting in the "ingredients" you want by being complimentary, sweet, gracious, supportive, friendly, and smiling. Remember your sacred space is a container. If only one of you puts in the sweet stuff, the contents will be sweeter; do your part without expectation or even hoping your spouse does his or her part.

The way to transcend the feelings of hurt and betrayal is by deciding you will. I will get into useful explanations in the lesson on the mind so you understand why the mind tends to remain attached to these harmful feelings. You can overcome the negative bonds. I will explain how you can get beyond those problem thoughts and feelings very quickly by choosing to control your mind.

Refuse to become intoxicated with being a victim. Don't imagine I just don't understand your particulars or you just can't do it. You would be setting yourself up for an even greater repeat of failed relationships. There are those among us who are overcome by the seeming immensity of the job of controlling the mind and freak out. But at some point the process must begin so that the pain ends. Your happiness is in your own hands.

Your particulars may be unique but the expression of love is the universal key to your happiness

I know it seems daunting to tackle seemingly impossible tasks, so I like to tell the story about my then five-year-old son who was told to clean up his room after it looked like it was hit by a hurricane. I said, "Joey, you need to clean your room." He looked at his room and burst into tears. I get a bit teary-eyed just recalling it. Isn't love so cool? It transcends space and time instantly with so much impact. I let him cry for a few seconds and when he grabbed my leg as a supplication for a reprieve, I took his hand and we stood on his bed.

I said, "Joey, I want you to tell me, what is the biggest thing you see on the floor?" (Which wasn't visible under the clutter, by the way). Between sobs, he pointed to his blanky. I said, "Go ahead, fold it up and put it in the closet." I did this forcefully to stave off the mental protests (we must be forceful with the mind). After he did this one task, I had him come back on the bed and look again. I repeated, "What is the biggest thing on the floor?" I can't remember the next object, but soon the room was well on its way to being clean. By breaking the job into manageable parts and going after the worst first, he soon had his room clean and life was back to normal.

It is up to you to stop your own unsavory behavior. The task of controlling the mind every time it resorts to the unhealthy habits of making a snide comment or giving a dirty look or dropping into self-pity is the most worthy effort you will ever make. It will change your life in all areas. In the meantime, though, seeing as we are human beings and not exactly perfect, even though we may know better, there are techniques we can use that will help us over the humps.

What if you slip sometimes? What if your partner slips?

What if the mudballs fly even though we try not to fling them?

I can assure you there will be slips no matter how hard you try (but still try very hard).

Say, "I'm sorry...I need to get a drink of water, may I get one for you?"

The above phrase, and its infinitely variable variations, is the most effective diffuser I am aware of. The first two words are the key. I'm sorry. Use them often!

You're going to slip. I guarantee it. Your spouse is going to slip. I guarantee it. When you slip or when your spouse slips, the most important thing is to stop the negative feelings from spiraling. You need to stop it very fast, as soon as you see things heading in a bad direction. **The most potent de-railer of negativity, the most effective diffuser, is to say, "I'm sorry."** You are not admitting guilt when you say this.

Each effort to control the mind brings us closer to "heaven"

You are sending a positive message of "Stop! Let's stop before we hurt each other. I love you!"

No matter how deeply you have gone and how out of control the conversation has gone, it is never too late to stop the flow. If the tension is high and you are both out of control (can happen!), the person who sees the insanity first is the one who should say it. Sometimes, especially in the beginning, it may be important to also physically disengage at the same time. Politely say something like, "Honey, I am out of control and I need to step back. It's not you, it's me. I'm sorry, and I must step back." Then physically slightly bow as you back out of the room, repeating, "I love you and I'm sorry." Mean it! Realize your mind has taken you on a path of pain and your spouse's words merely provided a trigger for your own hidden suffering to be released in a *convenient* form. Do not expect the same from your spouse. You can control only yourself. Be concerned only with your own behavior.

The above is the default circuit breaker. Use it! It must be used. It works and should be employed without fear. Don't hesitate. Use this prematurely rather than trying to get things back on track by some diplomatic means; it's safer. There is no issue worth losing your peace and relationship over.

If a bowling ball was coming at you full speed ahead (and sometimes those mudballs are just as hard as bowling balls) and you were a wall, that ball would hurt! Don't be a wall and don't be a target. If a bowling ball was coming at you full speed ahead and you were a feather, the ball would never even hit you. The wind force alone would send you floating in the air as the ball would harmlessly fly by. Be a feather!

Anyone can do what it takes. You can do it better!

How, you ask? The answer is, you direct your mind to recognize that your partner is in a bad way and you turn your self-pity (from being an attacked victim) into sympathy toward your erring spouse. It isn't crazy! The answer is taking control of your mind. The alternative is entering a cycle of reciprocating punches along with the drama and pain that really, really hurts. You are not responsible for your spouse's behavior, or anyone else's for that matter. Don't allow your mind to make your spouse's outbursts your fault or your problem. Whatever triggered it is just their problem, until you are triggered! Shifting perspective or reframing the situation will be most helpful.

I personally know someone who was in a very difficult divorce. Even after seven years, his ex-wife was doing everything she could to hurt my friend. She went after him in his professional world, through the courts, the school his child attended, and tried to harm his social life. She had so much unrestrained anger that she thought nothing about how her vindictiveness would hurt their child. She even used their child as a battleground by telling her that her father was evil and not really her father. For five years, my friend would confide his frustration and bounce his strategies off me, but all along, he was saying he wanted to transcend the situation and experience the feelings he was striving for, those of love and forgiveness. He had read an inspiring quote from St. Francis about forgiveness and believed he should be able to reach that saintly level of behavior in at least this one area. His battles with his mind were unbelievable and seemed at times to be almost impossible. He kept on and never gave up. Over time, he became notably changed.

My friend decided that his own flaws were not visible to him without the constant aggression that stimulated the bad thought habits he wanted to get rid of. He decided that without his ex-wife's behavior he would never have had the opportunity to work on his own flaws. He began to think of her as his best friend rather than his worst enemy. He reframed the situation so he could find peace in an otherwise disastrous set of circumstances.

After two years it became clear to me (and others) that his sincerity overcame his bad habit thoughts and he was making progress. He even wrote her a letter thanking her for playing that role in his life. He saw her role in a positive light and even saw her as unknowingly sacrificing her own peace. His attitude became one of gratitude and sympathy.

Though he still has to deal with her behavior, he does so with a perspective that is beneficial for his individual growth. He says that when he feels pain, it is clear to him that is the searchlight pointing out the mental decay in his own mind. Most importantly, he saved their daughter from being raised in the midst of a war.

Always see the pain as coming from your own weaknesses and know that the effort of working on your mind is vastly easier than living with weakness, which will chase you to the grave if you do not deal with it.

God knew we have flaws when he invented marriage. Those don't matter. We just have to follow the "rules for happiness".

Your children are natural recipients of your unconditional love, so you do not allow your *mind* (remember, your mind is a controllable tool, it is not you) to reduce your love for them; you control the mind, automatically stopping it from placing judgment ahead of love; I should say *eclipsing* love. You do not become stupidly unaware of the gravity of a bad deed. You simply refuse your judgments of their behavior to cross the line that separates your *mind* and its *reason* from your heart and its love. Controlling your mind is very good for all involved. Many of you, metaphorically, focus on a bit of trash that is floating on the ocean of love imagining the whole ocean to be irreversibly polluted. You promised to love in good times and bad when you got married; you promised!

Instead of making this all-inclusive and *self-preserving* promise a priority, you have allowed some *offense* (minor or major, it doesn't matter) to become more important than your commitment to love your spouse. The promise you made, which can be described as a reminder, to not become distracted by evil thoughts, is discarded at everyone's peril.

To illustrate the pettiness of the backward thinking we allow ourselves to slip into I clear the whiteboard in my office and make seven tiny point marks on the board. I then say to my clients, "These seven points represent each of your flaws (I don't know why I use seven, it just seems like a good number). The rest of the board plus the clear space on the other three walls represent your spouse's overall character."

Everyone agrees this is a fair illustration; our flaws in relation to our good qualities are pretty few and far between. I then point out the undisputable reality: no one is flawless. In addition, the flaws we focus on in each other are usually bothering us only because they are triggering our own peculiar weaknesses; some *flaws* simply don't bother us, while others are difficult for us to endure (flaws are in the eye of the beholder).

Pretend you are driving along on a sunny Sunday. You notice a beautiful lush lawn at a park and decide to have a picnic. You walk onto the lawn and you notice something "left there" that does not fit in with your initial image. Do you lay down your blanket by the "ugliness"? Do you pack up your stuff and leave? Do you find a nice spot away from the mess and complain about the offensive spot the whole time, ruining the picnic for everyone else? Or do you ignore the tiny bit of litter and talk about how lucky you are to have found such a beautiful lawn? Even the greatest masterpieces of art and music have flaws; this is planet Earth for God's sake. Nothing and nobody here is perfect. We love each other anyway.

Summary

• Your sacred space, just like your spouse, is of such high value that nothing compares; never abuse either.

• Make your behavior towards your spouse nothing short of reverent.

Your spouse is the most important person in your life…by far. The correct attitude to have is that you wish them to be happy. That does not mean to supply them with material wealth or outrageous gifts which only bring temporary excitement. It means to treat them with loving respect and kindness.

Always question your own behavior to see if it matches "the right thing to do".

Your marriage is a sacred space that shelters your family from the cruelties of the world. Always look for opportunities to contribute sweetness with sincere gestures.

The "rules" are designed around the structure of marriage and how individuals fit in best. As you try them you will see for yourself how easy it makes your marriage.

Why Men Act Like Men and Women Act Like Women

You are not your body; you have a body. The same is true about your mind. You are not your mind; you have one. Bodies have very strong drives, which completely control our mind in some cases and completely obscure our free thinking in others. When we understand these drives, called *psychophysiological imperatives**, we become much more in control of our mind and subsequent behaviors. It is not only possible but it is your obligation to intervene and have control over your mind. Like training a dog, the more you know about dogs the easier it is to train one. Similarly, when you understand these elements of the human body, you can better control your own behavior. You can have more self-control, compassion, less judgment, and no resentment toward your spouse's behaviors. By learning this simple science, you will understand so much.

The human body is on one level a biological organism that shares universal conditions of existence with its biological cousins. Even the most primitive life forms include in their makeup two primary drives. The first drive is for individual survival, which ensures existence to its own greatest capacity. Even single-cell organisms strive to survive (by being part of a protective community). The second drive, procreation, exists to ensure the continuation of the particular species. I am not aware of any living thing that does not have these two unseen qualities as part of its makeup.

The primary and strongest psychophysiological drive, survival, controls you in simple, subtle, and complex ways. Most of your

The body's two basic drives completely explains most behavior

You can trace almost every behavior to the body's requirements for survival and procreation

Your body is not your enemy; it just needs to be trained

---

* I have coined this phrase in order to succinctly convey the power of these overwhelming organic drives-PF

internal and external reactions are traceable back to this drive. The drive to survive triggers the mechanisms that protect the body and mind from imminent or future danger. If you are threatened by something that may hurt or end your body's life, all sorts of automatic reactions occur, such as the release of adrenalin and an immediate leap to *fight* or *flight* responses. The body and mind work together (physiological and psychological) to stop a threat or run from it, and they do it *now*. The inherent problem lies in interpreting what actually constitutes a life-threatening event. How much of one is operating instinctively like an animal or using wisdom and self-control varies greatly with each of us. But there are certain events that probably get the same response from almost everyone. Imagine, for instance, what might happen if someone were to walk over to you and try to plug your nose and block your mouth. You would not allow it! Every bodily and mental resource would jump in to prevent the possibility of your death.

The drive to survive exaggerates threats when not countered by practical analysis

Unfortunately, the culturalized mind categorizes some events that are not actually life threatening as if they are (like the termination of a job or an insult from an important person in your life) and creates all the bodily and psychological reactions that would normally be reserved for the real thing, like increased heart rate and rapid breath, defensive posturing, etc. The mind may push you to avoid the perceived death traps with lies and evasions, hiding facts that seem to increase the perceived threat. Misclassifying something as a life threat is the cause of distress and ongoing stress. Use common sense to distinguish real threats from a bump in the road. Don't just accept your automatic responses. Calmly evaluate what you are facing, so your mind doesn't just shift to its most primal response. It is up to you to "stop the action."

The range of possible responses extends from going berserk to being Gandhi-like. A person might go berserk because someone looked at them funny, which threatens their manhood or womanhood, thus their survival. A person may respond like Gandhi, who was undisturbed when a man shot him to death (a well-documented historical fact, demonstrating his extraordinary level of self-control). In the first case, there is a short circuit from threat to reaction. In the second example, Gandhi disciplined his mind to ignore the automatic signals; everything he encountered he analyzed. He chose, by filtering the information through his trained mind, an appropriate response rather than allowing an automatic reaction. Gandhi's is the ultimate behavior.

During a prize fight, a champion boxer bit off the ear of his opponent. He said he was not aware of it at the time. Despite rejection of his contention by many skeptics, you can now see he may have been telling the truth. His life seemed so threatened that his conscious mind completely shut down; nothing but animal instincts remained in charge of his behavior.

In most of us, the triggers for survival defenses are all over the map, rarely based on truly threatening situations, just odd habits picked up over time from various situations and never consciously sorted out (like a fixated fear of dogs). Now is the time to take responsibility for your behavior instead of acting out of instinct. You can stop your auto-responses when you want to control them even though they are biologically driven at the core. You will prove to yourself your ability to take control as soon as you try to. The trick is to stop your automatic reactions immediately when you see them, then apply reason to the current situation. The triggers and levels of intensity will be different for everybody. The things that trigger you are generally known as your hot buttons, and they need to be removed one by one. Just because they have a cute little name, *hot buttons*, doesn't make them cute at all. Turn them in to *not* buttons. Watch them get pushed. Disconnect them by forcing yourself to evaluate what just happened instead of allowing your mind and body to jump into unthinking action.

It is also critical to be aware of your spouse's struggles with psychophysiological drives. When your spouse reacts intensely to something, it is wise and kind to remember his or her area of sensitivity so you can avoid striking the nerve that sends a message of danger. That makes sense, right? If someone has a sprained wrist, you wouldn't ask that person to help move a piano, would you? The psychological sensitivity is theirs, so you don't want to excite it or comment on it, but you can certainly avoid bringing discomfort to them or even relieve some of their pain by being sweet and comforting.

On the other hand, it is wise to note your own automatic reactions to your spouse's reactions so that you can recalibrate your sensitivities to calmer and more realistic levels. If you fly off the handle because your spouse didn't ask for your help in the way you

Controlling the mind brings peace

Turn your *hot* buttons into *not* buttons.

expected, it is a good idea to stop your own reactive explosion dead in its tracks. You don't need to know why you were trained to fly off the handle; it is just a bad habit that needs to be replaced with a good habit. It is an utter waste of time going back to your past to discover when you became sensitive; it does not help. Who knows when you began hearing an otherwise ordinary phrase as a call to arms? Maybe when you were a kid you felt scared when your mom said something, and it was coincidentally followed by a meteor hitting your house missing you by four inches! Who cares; the associated fear was lodged in there and now it needs to be dislodged—no big deal! The phrase your mom used has a subconscious relationship to panic response and needs to be deintensified through will power. Knowing its origin doesn't help you dislodge it. Unless you are under the influence of drugs (including alcohol and certain medication) or have a serious mental disease, you have all the power you need to change your reactions. Some take more effort and more time—you have to start sometime.

Bear in mind your reactions will become hotter as your triggers are hit more often, like a nerve getting more and more sensitive. So, if you are the hitter, you need to back off when you see your spouse getting caught in a psychological trap. It appears so easy for them to overcome it from your safe perspective, but you are not there for that. Alternately, when you are the hittee, you need to step back from yourself. Explain to yourself that you are actually safe. Remember, be only your own teacher, never your spouse's.

Reducing your sensitivities by using wisdom-guided will is the most effective effort you can make. When you catch yourself reacting out of habit to some odd stimulant (like your spouse telling you a hair is out of place), merely stop and say "I'm sorry." After you make sure your spouse is okay, go on (no big deals), or disengage for a time and recall how much you love your spouse and how wonderful he or she is.

Make your impulses trigger consideration rather than reaction

A huge area of concern these days is body weight. There seems to be a new diet every month, and most of them work only for a short time. Diets don't work because people do not understand what eating is all about.

When diets fail, everyone says something like, "I just can't stick with it," or "I lack the will power." In most cases, the weak link is not in the diet or will power. It is more accurate to say there is a lack of correct application of will power. The desire to eat comes from survival instincts.

The body drives the desire for food in order to survive. If we don't eat, we won't live. Unfortunately, we follow hunger signals from the body as if they were commands. When we get a hunger signal we think we have to eat. We don't consider the body's purposeful systems, the reasons for the stimulations. For instance, when the eyes see a food source, it lets the mind know sustenance is available (the eyes don't discriminate between the nutritional values of different edibles—we allow commercials to do that). If it's the last food source for five days or something that information is critical to survival. The mind converts the message of availability to hunger, even though it should have just said there was an opportunity. The mind's efficiency (another two edged blade) goes right to "feed the body." The mind sends signals to the stomach and mouth and we actually experience hunger not induced by an actual need for nutrition.

In the case of a normal sequence, the cells put out a call for nutrients, and the discriminative part of the mind decides the signal is based on actual need and responds accordingly. The palate now selects foods that will take care of the need, acting as a guarded gate by deciding what is useful and what is not, what is nutritional and what is not. But that doesn't happen.

Use your discrimination to determine if the body should eat and store more nutrition, or if it has plenty and should wait. We think we are hungry just because the palate says food is available. Instead of regulating the intake, we stop using the mind's power of discrimination and get fat even though we are only eating when we are "hungry." We short circuit, the process at our health's peril. Another problem is we stop choosing (if we ever did) foods based on their usefulness to the body. We barely discern between cream-filled chocolate and fresh green salad. The mind shouts *hungry* and we eat what is tasty and convenient.

Don't listen to the faddist expression "listen to your body" in the context of commands, like a dog listening to its master. You are the master of your body, not the other way around. Make it listen to you. Just pay attention to real needs by using your discrimination. If the body is sending false alarms, shut it up. Or, if you can't

Don't allow your body's drives to push you around

99% of what you perceive as a threat is not—just smile and say "I love you." Then evaluate the "threat"

muster the discipline at that moment (it can be tough to beat back a strong habit), satisfy the craving with something that won't add to your dietary problems. However, never mentally give in by making excuses; that will set you back. I like the expression, "If you have to go into the bar, take God in there with you." Don't pretend it is not happening. Keep your awareness honest and live through the weakness. Tomorrow is another day and you will not be perfect in one try. Never give up!

In your relationship, responses pop up when you misread signals. When you feel attacked it is because your survival instincts tell you your very survival is threatened and then your imagination (designed to create solutions, not elaborate threats) pushes you to your limits. Although you may have modified your defensive attacks so that you don't chop off the attacker's head, recognize that innocent events are turned into attacks by the drive to survive; you overreact. Ninety-nine percent of what you perceive as an attack is not; no response of any kind, other than a smile (because you love your spouse so much) is required or appropriate.

The same naturally beneficial response of jumping out of the way when a speeding car is veering toward you is likewise triggered indiscriminately when your spouse says something that, for some psychological reason, creates a sense of imminent danger. It is important to understand this inappropriate response so you can catch your mind in the act of trying to scare you.

Imagination is a great tool for creating solutions

The survival switch (still known as the panic button) hits all the smaller switches and jams the body and mind into hyper drive. After all, the mind is "dumb" and does only what it is used to doing. It stems from the body's need to survive. Because we have allowed our reactions to be automatic, the effect is powerful. It's like smashing a light bulb instead of taking the time to walk over to the wall switch; it's like jumping fifteen feet to douse the candle flame with water instead of walking over and snuffing it with your finger tips.

When the mind has mistakenly perceived an experience as life threatening all your responses will jolt you into a mindless tactical effort designed to protect your body from imminent danger and you end up offending everyone with a paranoid reaction. It is important to be in control of your mental and physical realms. We are back to the same major point: it is your mind, and you need to control it or be controlled by it; the choice is yours.

When the drive for survival is unregulated and responds to the uncontrolled imagination's interpretation of danger, it is freak-out city.

Methods such as deep, slow breathing, which pushes more oxygen into the brain and slows the heart rate, will stop automatic processes dead in their tracks. Then speak to yourself (your mind) about how silly its reaction is. Even if your mind seems so out of control that you can't think of a technique at the moment bear in mind you must ultimately gain control; there is no other way. **It is *your* mind and body, and it is *your* responsibility to control them.** Don't be satisfied with a little temporary relief.

Psychologists have slipped into the mode of thinking you must go through decades of therapy to *cure* this problem. That's because psychologists make a living (survival) out of regular weekly sessions. Are they not victims, too, who thrive on others in order to survive? I point this out so you can see how insidious the untrained and improperly managed mind is. Psychologists aren't evil people, you know. Most are basically decent folks who start out because they are frightened by their minds and need some understanding. Most become psychologists because they feel better from Freudian explanations and believe they can bring some relief to other folks, even when they are inwardly confused.

Start paying attention! Slow down the movie! Own your destiny!

The body drives the mind, and the mind tells the body what to do. These parts of you work without supervision; they are just habits. Jump back into the driver's seat. If you don't drive your vehicle in life, someone or something else will.

The Procreative Drive

Women are "designed," biologically and psychologically, to carry a newly conceived human until it is ready to leave the womb, then feed and protect the dear child until it is ready for an independent life. Psychological and physiological mechanisms compel women to love and nurture. Though mitigated by cultural prerogatives, these drives are extremely powerful, as every woman will attest.

Women's physical procreative drives seem further complicated by her needs for survival (the first imperative). A woman's needs for security are well known. Because she is designed to protect her

The *procreative drive* is the one that gives people the most trouble in their relationships

offspring at all costs, she requires a secure environment. It is fair to say a woman's need for security is as powerful as a man's need for sex.

A woman is biologically *driven* to copulate only once a cycle, only for a few hours. Her procreative drives manifest in the following ways with tremendous importance—preening, mate selecting, nesting, fertilizing, nurturing.

Men are driven to protect and copulate. Those men who stray are mindlessly heeding their body's drive to copulate. If a man was walking across a minefield and was blown in half, the part with the penis would still be ready for sex. As a woman walks by and innocently smiles, he would say, "What's up? Are you busy?" even as his blood and life-force are rushing out of his body. The male must be ready 24/7, so he won't miss a rare opportunity; lest the species would die off (notice how I, a man, use a *violent* example—the man is the protector and incorporates violence because it is required at times).

Natural drives are only considered intrusive or unloving when they are misunderstood.

So, men, now you know why there are so many headaches. Women are far less psychophysiologically driven to have raw sex; the woman's psychophysiological imperative for raw sex only occurs monthly and then only lasts a few hours. The "other" (which manifest quite differently) reasons for women to have needs for intimacy are *indirectly* compelling and are just as valid, and still line up with males' needs. The few women who find themselves driven to the sex act as often as men have overridden their biological imperatives for *other* reasons (which still trace back to psychophysiological imperatives). Lining up your desires is very sweet. When the needs of your spouse are understood and not condemned both husband and wife find regular fulfillment comes naturally.

So, women, now you know why he seems to be so obsessed with sex. If he was only willing to have intercourse as often as your body needs, it might never happen because of timing issues and there would be no more human race. His body is forcing his mind to come up with all sorts of reasons why he should have sex and his mind is accommodating to any proposal you may come up with. Then he is faced with all kinds of "trouble" for following his *inner* guidance system. Does this mean either spouse should now accommodate the other's *drives* without regard for self? The answer is yes and no. This topic is covered in the last lesson in ways that have proven to be more than satisfactory for most couples. At this point all I suggest is that you remove the judgments and criticisms by understanding that neither of you are cold or perverted.

Women and men can choose not to be defined by their psychophysiological drives. As free beings we may rise above bodily requirements. We are not destined to be slaves to our bodies, but we are not entirely free, either. By being aware of innate physical *drives*, we can discern our real motivations better; and using our discrimination, we can live with less internal conflict. We can make choices that respond to outer and inner stimulation with an awareness of why we seem compelled beyond our best inner judgments. Being consciously aware of these drives mitigates judgment, guilt, and frustration. It explains the occasional weirdness without *excusing* it. It allows us to be more compassionate toward our spouse and ourselves when behaviors come up that are not what we would normally expect.

Behave according to higher principles (to the best of your ability) which will define you as a wonderful spouse regardless of how your spouse behaves.

A natural and satisfying bridge exists (last lesson)

Things to Remember

For Women

Your husband is not a "dog". He does love you and does care about your feelings. On the other hand he cannot just dismiss the drives which often overshadow all reason. Your compassion and understanding must replace judgment and criticism. Satisfying your husband while showing him the "love" part of making love will satisfy both of you.

For Men

Your wife will never respond to being berated. Respond to her needs to be taken seriously as a woman by loving, listening and adoring her. Your wife is not there to get you off. Very few women are satisfied by non loving sex. It merely frustrates them and makes them feel empty.

For Both

Intimacy is one of the cornerstones of a healthy marriage. No matter how long it has been since you have slept together or how afraid you are of trying again don't dismiss the possibilities for an amazing relationship that includes amazing intimacy.

The last lesson completes this lesson but you should not skip to it. There is still foundational ground to cover.

The Reason We Get Married

> **You can greatly enhance the joy of marriage when you know why you got married**

When my wife and I were newly married, I playfully asked her why she married me. Her response was, "Because you're cute." Later on after we had gone through some years and our life was stable, I asked her the same question. Her answer was, "Because you're cute and I always knew you would be successful" (physical attraction plus security). Much later, almost twenty years, as we were going through our pre-divorce difficulties, I asked her the same question. The last time I asked, it was not really a question per se, it was more of a challenge (I was not feeling very loved and respected). Her snappy answer was actually very honest: "I have no idea." Of course, I was still cute and I was still successful, but obviously the original *reasons* were not of the enduring variety.

Had my wife and I known what I know now... For most people marriage is an inevitable part of life we all look forward to. The questions we typically ask are "Who should I marry? Who will marry me?" and/or "How many kids should we have?" We look around, date, get to know someone we are relatively comfortable with, do a little testing of each other's character (too little), and start planning our marital future.

We generally get all excited, somewhat relieved, and a little scared during the stage of life when we are ready to find a mate. Very few of us talk or think about why we want to marry—I mean, really, there is a lot to consider! People rarely actually list what is important to them or how a spouse is going to contribute to their happiness. There is a grand assumption that everything will work out because "love conquers all." This is (more than coincidentally) good thinking when we understand the mechanics of marriage. The expectation is realistic, just not as we initially imagine. In the meantime, most folks can list some very good and honest reasons when asked why they want to be married. As you

Always behave in a way that reminds your spouse of the reasons they were first attracted to you

may suspect, the top answers are different by gender; but there is a grand purpose or two for getting married, which is the result of our needing to fulfill our destinies. Our destinies are prescribed by our physical and spiritual requirements.

It is fascinating; you arrived at the most important decision you will ever make with relatively little knowledge, understanding, or planning. When you remodel your kitchen (a mundane task in comparison to getting married), you do an enormous amount of research. You take pains to ensure your choices reflect your desired use of the space and your personal taste. Every detail is important, and the outcome reflects your needs, desires, emotions, and thoughtfulness—everything has to be perfect. Most people put more time and effort into planning a wedding reception than the marriage itself. Our culture does not prescribe any practicality in this area. Our focus is on romance and sex appeal, the least important factors over the long run. Most couples are not remotely aware of the most basic values they share (or disagree about) because they have avoided any communication that may cause disharmony. (Remember *The Newlywed Game* on TV?) We must also admit we had no idea what it means to be married when we got married. At the time, we only had a vague notion of waking up next to our true love and best friend, beginning our days with smiles and supportive loving words, and maybe sex. We imagined being listened to, cared for, loved, supported, sexually satisfied, and more. All our expectations were positive—and primarily selfish. So please step back and ask the question, What do *I* want from my marriage?

In my private sessions, I asked couples to go back in time and say what they expected from their upcoming marriage when they stepped down the aisle. They could pretend to remember if their mind was drawing a blank or if they had no conscious expectations. There are no wrong answers. Current answers are as valid as ten-year-old answers. Due to burnout most said they only wanted peace, a break from hostilities. But I made them go back to the starry-eyed moments just before the fears leading up to their vows. (By this time, all the couples vowed to end their hostilities and we proceeded to proactive positives.) The answers I received were consistent for the most part. If you were to list all the things you want from your relationship, the list would probably be similar to what I heard and it would likely include the following:

- Companionship

- Best friend

- Trust

- Respect

- Children

- Security (number one for most women)

- Sex (number one for most men)

Can you see how this list so neatly lends itself to fulfilling the psychophysiological requirements discussed in the previous lesson? Although friendship (which some said is spiritual, not physiological) is a spiritual quality, it is founded in a need caused by physiological drives. The preceding chapter focuses on the physical, but the same patterns of hidden drives exist on the spiritual plane as well. As invisible physiological drives compel us to think and act in ways that will fulfill survival and procreation, so a hidden spiritual drive is also operative. And just because we can't test tube these drives and qualities does not mean they are not there. And just because Western psychologists imagine psychology is devoid of God doesn't mean they are correct.

There is a barely hidden psychospiritual drive called Divine Love. The one reliable link we have with God is love. Love is so far beyond emotion that it is actually a misnomer to call love an emotion. It is more accurate to say love can spark emotion and vice-versa. The point is that love is God and God is love. When you are feeling love, you are experiencing God; it is unparalleled in its effect upon us and indefinable by the mind. It is simple. It is pure. It is needed universally. The need for love is so great that it scares the unreligious (who think they control things) into the futile act of trying to understand it. It is not understandable by the mind. Therefore, our society has not analyzed how it all ties together.

God loves you. He (or She) loves you in ways unimaginable. God also loves you to the same degree as His other most noble children. You have allowed yourself to be distracted from God as you continue to get wrapped up in His creation, but God loves you too much to let you get away completely. He planted in your heart,

Giving love as unconditionally to your spouse as you can is safe; it is the whole idea of marriage

in every particle of your heart, a craving for His Divine Love. So even though you have become engrossed in body and mind in His creation (He designed the compelling psychophysiological imperatives), yet He tipped the scales with the spiritually implanted need for Divine Love. You, your spouse, myself, and everyone else has a hidden powerful need for Divine, or *unconditional, love.*

I know the above may sound absurdly simple (compared to getting married due to cuteness, for instance). **Your own primary reason for getting married was to receive unconditional love.** The above is not the *only* reason to get married. Obviously, there are the physiological psychological and emotional reasons. But by focusing on improving your ability to give and receive love, you create a win-win situation that honors all the God-instilled drives: physical, psychological, and spiritual.

This is probably the single most important thing you will learn for gaining real happiness:

The science of love is worth learning. The great among us (Mother Theresa comes to mind) discovered the scientific laws of love and lived them despite worldly temptations and pressures to abandon their commitments to loving others ahead of themselves. They discovered love to be the ultimate everything. They also discovered love is God's, and is God. Love does not come from any other source—it comes only from God. So when you are feeling love from someone, it is actually God loving you through that person. The person who is giving you love is actually providing a channel for God so that He can love you through them. You are actually serving God by being His channel.

When you give love, you are actually feeling His love pouring through you; *and* it is way easier to feel love flow through you in this act of giving. Giving love is the easiest way to get love. I do not mean that by giving love someone will be compelled to love you in return! You see, the love you give is flowing through you from God to the person you are loving. You are tasting the love that is flowing through you in a greater measure than the person for whom that love is intended. This is the greatest of all secrets. If you ask yourself whether you have felt more love—by giving it or getting it—you will find from your own recollection the experience

The supreme reason to get married is to gain unconditional love

of *giving* love is far more powerful and satisfying. Try it right now and see. Feel love from someone who you are convinced loves you (who may not be *loving you* at this precise moment; that won't affect this experiment). Next, give love to someone whom you truly love. I know you will experience much greater love when you are *giving love*; it is not even close! This little experiment has the same repeatable result no matter who tries it; making the experiment *scientific*. Giving love is the best way to feel love.

Now that you have made your lists, I am willing to wager you did not include the *real reason* you wanted to be married at all. Of all the reasons that may be listed, there is one that stands supreme (yet only three people of all I met with ever listed it).

Is it not true? In the back of your mind, **don't you want to be loved unconditionally? Wasn't that an unspoken expectation? Is it not painful that it's not happening?** It's crazy! You never discussed it or quantified it. You never identified it as missing or present. Yet, **if you experience unconditional love, nothing else will matter.** You could be destitute, sick, struck by tragedy or anything else; if you have unconditional love, you have it all. You will think of yourself as the most fortunate person in the world. **What we want and need most is unconditional love.** The greatest craving we have from marriage or anywhere else is for unconditional love. The need for unconditional love is in our very soul and must be satisfied.

But, alas, it cannot be satisfied through human love. A mother's love (found in fathers, too) comes very close, (well kind of—it sort of mimics God's love). However, when we define unconditional love in its broadest sense wherein we are completely loved, never judged, always understood, and loved eternally, we realize even a mother's love falls short (mothers die, for instance). The thought of being loved *unconditionally* by a spouse is *completely* unrealistic. We are, after all, *human*. Yet, we have a powerful innate drive, demanding fulfillment. Logic dictates the one place God would have us fulfill the deepest need we have (which He created) is in marriage. Right? Yet *no spouse* can give it to us. What gives? Please think about this. Isn't your desire for unconditional love the main reason *you* wanted to be married? Isn't this your core expectation?

We get love when we give it. This explanation is practical and scientific.

Look at this a bit more closely. **The need for unconditional love is clearly built in every one of us; not feeling loved is at the root of every trouble and sorrow.** God endowed us with this need. Then, he made it impossible for us to *receive it* from our spouse. **But we *can* get unconditional love, by _giving it_ to our spouse. We get love when we give it.** This explanation is practical and scientific.

The exclusive and original source of all love is God. As humans, we are not able to *create* or generate love; we cannot even properly define it, much less break it down into components and produce it. But we know love exists by how it *feels*. We also know from our own past individual experience that giving love creates a greater experience of love than *receiving* love (the exception to this is when we become aware of God's love through devotional practices such as deep prayer, meditation, and other forms of proactive communion). When we *give* love, we are actually opening ourselves as channels for *God's* ever flowing love. The reason we feel more love by giving love is because we receive it directly from the source in order to pass it on, rather than by getting it from another human "distributer" which is blocked and filtered by *human* fears. By becoming a channel of God's love, you are experiencing that which is flowing through you. When you try to give love unconditionally, you won't suffer from the mind's limitations (fear, doubt, envy, etc.). By focusing the mind (it's *your* mind, and you can tell it what to do) on giving love to your partner, along with love's manifestations of respect, admiration, devotion, and loyalty, you will feel the love you have always sought. Use the tools of the mind—will power, imagination, and discrimination—to zero in on this effort.

> **By being a channel for God's love, you are experiencing that which is flowing through you**

This is the "heart" of the lessons. Love your spouse unconditionally to the best of your ability and you will benefit in ways unimaginable. Your marriage will be amazing, and your life will be even better.

This works for everyone. The effort required is miniscule compared to the benefits, so even if your efforts slip a little, if you resume the effort nothing will be lost. You want unconditional love and this is how you get it. You will also get the most incredible marriage in the process. It is so simple and flawless.

Make a vow to try this for a period of time and then stick to it. **Always look for and take advantage of opportunities to express unconditional love towards your spouse.** After a short time span, like twenty-four hours, you can renew your vow again... and again until your mind gives way to your heart, until you are again living in joyful matrimony.

Forget the adages about not going to sleep without making up—don't get in a fight. Treat your spouse in ways that make her or him want you forever.

I have seen folks who have gone through hell so long they couldn't tell which way was up; all they wanted was a marriage they could *tolerate*. You are good people who love your spouses, but just didn't know how to make it work. But when you love unconditionally you go from pain and suffering to bliss in such a short time you will almost beg me to tell you it won't work forever—like those who tried before you. But it does! It just keeps getting better and better.

You need to give love the way you want to feel it: unconditionally. You need to receive love in the way that stimulates more: with gratitude. You can quickly reverse the downward spiral of bad feelings which create more bad feelings by becoming *good* regardless of your partner's efforts or lack thereof. The love you seek is yours once you realize it comes from within, where God is, not from your spouse.

Change your behavior. Make this commitment and it will immediately change everything about your marriage. This is perhaps the greatest secret of success. When you apply yourself to this, alone, giving unconditional love in as many ways as you can imagine, you will be happy—guaranteed!

At this point, the "yeah but" birds come in full force. Shoo those rascals away! Unconditional love expresses love without expecting anything in return. You must let go of your desires for compensation and recognition for your efforts and achievements. Even though your mind will clearly tell you how you are being stupid for your efforts ignore its selfishness. You will feel empowered if you recognize your struggle as a war against detrimental thoughts and habits instead of a battle against your spouse's flaws.

This is the greatest secret of success: if you apply yourself to giving unconditional love in as many ways as you can imagine, you will be happy.

Give unconditional love in order to feel unconditional love

Okay, this is not always easy—I know! This topic is the one I have gotten the most phone calls about after couples were on the right track. The pattern of the call was always the same. The caller would tell me about an offense and ask me what to do. My answer was always a question: are you expressing unconditional love? Are you being compassionate instead of defensive? It is tough to fight the fear (of the mind) but it is the way! The key to success is in working with *human nature,* avoiding suffering. It may seem, at first glance, like the effort to love unconditionally is beyond your capability; I even supplied ammunition by telling you it is impossible for us to do so. So here is the rule of thumb I want you to always remember: it will serve you in many areas of your life. Ready?

The effort required to do the right thing, no matter how great, in order to avoid suffering, is miniscule compared to the suffering that comes from not doing (or trying to do) the right thing.

Always treat your spouse as the most important person in your life. Everything will be fine when you remember to love your spouse with all you have and show it in ever more creative ways.

Earth will always be Earth; but if you behave like an angel, you will have heaven on Earth.

Do's and Don'ts

Do love your spouse with all your might

Do see your spouse's flaws with compassion

Do say "I love you" often and with sincerity (at least 3 times a day)

Do compliment your spouse often (at least 3 times a day)

Do adore your spouse

Do tell your spouse they are handsome or beautiful every day

Do respect your spouse in words, deeds and thoughts

Do keep track of your efforts and successes

Do look for opportunities to make your spouse feel special

Don't criticize your spouse (ever)

Don't take another's side against your spouse (ever)

Don't lie to your spouse

Don't say anything that might be hurtful

Don't give up no matter how difficult the moment

Many readers found Lesson Ten to be the most valuable of all the lessons for within these pages you will find simple common sense explanations of the mind's architecture and how to make it work for you. For those who have been inundated by Freudian nonsense it is suggested you do not attempt to dovetail the two distinct approaches. After all, the reason to study the mind is to achieve happiness. The Freudian model, rejecting "Intelligent guidance" (God), is a primitive "religion" which relies on farfetched beliefs. Our scientific model gives anyone the ability to be their own psychologist and thus create their own destiny. You don't need to suffer any more.

Great changes will be in store for those who accept the fact that not only can you place your mind under your control, but you are obligated to do so.

The Mind

*T*hink of your mind as a computer, engineered with unparalleled efficiency and simplicity to be your most valuable servant. The mind is your possession. You most definitely have the ability to control your mind. You also have the obligation to do so. You are able to observe your mind. You can watch *yourself* think, feel, sort thoughts and feelings, and even determine which thoughts and feelings you wish to entertain and which you wish to keep out. Because of your power over your mind, you have many choices; but most people don't take it seriously or even think about it. Most people in the world think they are who they are and that's that. The truth is you have infinite control over who you are and what you will become even in the next instant. It is the choices you make about which thoughts you will entertain, and the resultant actions, that define you.

Thoughts and feelings are two sides of one coin. They do not originate within the mind. Thoughts are in the ether, much like radio and television signals, undetectable without a properly tuned receiver. The mind picks up primarily thoughts that are aligned with root habits of thinking. If someone is a bank robber, they pick up thoughts about banks, getaway cars, and guns; whereas a fashion model will pick up thoughts about hair, shoes, and diet plans. If a model wants to become a jet pilot, they need only retune their minds by willful direction. If someone wishes to change their thinking, all they need to do is apply will power to the process. When a thought comes to mind that one does not wish, one can reject it. Although the first thought of a particular topic will come because of a habit or some momentary influence, you have the ability to reject it and refuse future similar thoughts. Thoughts can

Fear and caution are not degrees of the same thing. Fear is a disease.

actually be exchanged or replaced; not changed. You have to reject the ones you don't want. Then you have to replace the unwanted thoughts with thoughts that are more beneficial.

Thoughts and feelings bring about various moods; various states of mind induce different thoughts and feelings; it is a cycle. Until you step in and consciously change the track of thoughts and feelings, you are the victim of a runaway mind. In modern society, most people unconsciously derail unwanted trains of thoughts and feelings by putting their attention on some form of *entertainment* like TV, music, conversation or other mind occupiers. This isn't bad, of course, but it would be better if you acknowledged that you did not like where the mind was going and turned it toward productive feelings and thoughts of love, service, or creativity. Other people derail their thinking with a glass of wine or mixed drink, which reduces "will power"—the "tool" you need most.

If your mind "bites" it is up to you to train it—just as you would your dog

There are powerful enemies of the mind like fear and anger that have more power than you realize. These two demon emotions are not internally produced, but like all thoughts and feelings, can only harm you and others when allowed access and residence. In other words, you do not have to get to the bottom of the particulars of why you are feeling fear and anger in order to dispatch them. They are held by habitual tendencies that can be overridden. When I first recognized this reality, I tried to push out anger by repeating over and over, "anger get out" and found no success (there are those who do find success with that method—I just lacked the will power). I was stripping my internal gears with the effort. I discovered there was no easy way for me to eradicate anger (my particular nemesis), but I also began to see how much of my life was short-changed because of its presence. I had to better understand its nature. For more knowledge and strategies, I turned to Eastern psychology.

The first thing I learned is: anger comes when we don't get our way (i.e. we open the door and invite anger in). Some say they "use" anger as a tool (talk about making a deal with the devil!) The habitual tendencies conducive to anger are all about rigidity of thoughts and ideas. By thinking we know all the answers we are ill prepared to listen to and value the ideas and/or feelings of others. We think ideas or behavior that run contrary to our thinking are an intrusion (the thought of an intrusion also invites anger in).

In my own case I realized my habitual attitudes of over-self-assuredness were like candy to anger. I had to reevaluate and change them. Everyone can develop their own system to break the cycle and I share mine only as an example :

My personal system to combat anger

> When I first become angry, I put the mental brakes on as soon as I notice. No matter what is happening I mentally step back so anger is no longer driving me. If I have to, I disengage from the interaction, because the last thing I want to do is stimulate someone else's anger.
>
> Next, I remind myself that anger is not going to bring me peace—not now, not later, not eventually, not ever! I then instruct my mind to look for a solution that is noble even if I lack the self-control to implement it. By tasking my mind, I am shifting its attention to something productive instead of destructive and giving myself a goal of behaving in a way I know is better. I also remind myself that everything comes from God, and I should be grateful for seeing my weaknesses so I can work on them; instead of throwing a tantrum because it didn't go the way I wanted it to. I also have done some long deep breathing when I have been really fuming. The last thing I do is not give up. I keep explaining to myself why anger is useless and destructive and appeal to my higher reason until anger is no longer an option.

My personal remedy for fear is similar. I appeal to my higher reason—I talk *to* myself, I talk *at* myself—until I pay attention and shift my thinking away from demon fear. I also use comparisons to convince myself that my idea of danger is *foolish* based on the very real plights of a gazillion other people around the world. Never justify fear or anger; neither can ever serve your interests.

I have experienced notable progress in my own war with fear and anger. One of my favorite techniques is to remind myself that no other person has control over my behavior. If my current "adversary" wants to act like an idiot and I act like an idiot back to them, I have

The system you employ will work over time and even be improved over time- never give up

effectively handed them control over my behavior. The second part of that is to be inwardly grateful to them for exposing my own soft spots. If not for them I would think I am perfect. Everyone in this world is either fighting or giving in to fear and anger. That's just what lives here with us (along with rats, mosquitoes, viruses, and other enemies of man). Just because fear and anger are not visible, per se, does not mean they are not our enemy. We can't see viruses and bacteria either! Don't give up. Do all you can to fight off this vermin by keeping alert and steady.

Fear and anger are selfish expressions and poison your marriage if you allow them to. When your spouse is caught by these two evil sisters, see your spouse as a victim and don't take his or her meanness personally. If you can't filter what is coming at you, it is better to mentally step out of range and try to be nice so you do not become infected too. Don't say something like, "I see you are feeling angry," because that is a condemnation. Ignore the anger and the fear. An unnoticed guest will soon leave. Definitely avoid thoughts of superiority and wanting to help—you cannot! Each of us has our battles and we must face them. You can be supportive and compassionate. In fact, as a spouse, it is your privilege to be supportive and compassionate. It looks something like, "I think I understand where you are coming from and, as usual, you have given me a new and maybe better way to look at things. Thank you. It would be better for me to let what you have said settle in, and maybe now is not the best time to discuss this. What do you think?"

The suggestions I pass on to you work, but don't impose upon yourself implementation of every nuance and method. Most of this is inspiration for you to prime your own pump. A happy marriage of mutual adoration and service is natural. The other kind of marriage is not normal.

Free Will and Habits

It is very useful to understand habits. Habit is the ultimate time saver and efficiency "program". When we do not consciously choose our habits, they become great enemies. Habit is the autopilot of the mind. It allows us to walk, talk, run, throw, dance, ride a bike, bake, respond to the doorbell, and virtually everything else without having to think through what the next steps are. When a habit is beneficial, we are able to roll on to our next event or task while our attention is on other things. It frees up our ability to be creative and productive. Unfortunately, it also allows us to throw away our time in front of television and waste our time on useless distractions.

Our free will decides what we do only when employed. You are either using your free will to fashion habits or habits are controlling you, thus stealing your free will. The worst habits are the ones that have us repeating destructive thoughts, feelings, and behaviors without scrutiny—long-standing habits form actual grooves in our brain. They become so much a part of us that if they are not beneficial we have a very tough time removing them.

The secret to habit removal is habit replacement. If you have a habit of being critical, the fastest way to eliminate it is to look for opportunities to praise. If you have the habit of seeing the cup half empty, make it a point to see the cup full of bounty. Let's say you are looking at the traffic in front of you and it is jammed up. Normally you might be prone to getting negative. But instead you look up a bit and notice the beautiful sky that is there despite the traffic. Now you think about how beautiful the sky is and keep the train of your thoughts on the beauty expanding to outer space and the stars, or birds and sweet nature. This effort will erode the habit of negative thinking and at the same time begin to establish a new habit.

The way you treat your spouse is also habitual. In the case of reforming habits, you have a definite advantage as a married couple. You see a lot of what influences your behavior and thoughts is the environment you are in. When you are at work, you are habituated to have certain kinds of thoughts about work. When you are on a playing field, you tend to have associated thoughts about competitive sports. The differing influences extend into all sorts of areas—cemeteries, churches, schools, weddings, train stations, airports, and more. Differing associations influence and trigger different trains of thought. Well, your marriage is a sacred space and has unique associations. It is up to you to recall the more beautiful associations of your marriage, the ones that got you to be married in the first place, and willfully keep those thoughts center stage until they become habit again.

It is only because "worldly" thought habits came into your sacred space when you "slipped" that things changed. Now they have become temporarily entrenched in your relationship. Once you establish the habits of thinking about your spouse with continual respect and adoration and completely cease all mudball launches, it will be relatively easy to maintain them. Sweet habits for your sacred space will positively distinguish your marriage relationship from the rest of the world. It is like how your habits are different when you are in a church rather than at your job so you don't have to think "I am in a church" the whole time. It's just how you train your mind.

Habits are triggered by different causes. You have to make sure your relationship is positively unique in your mind so your good habits do the work of "remembering" for you. Make it a habit to think of your relationship as being a sacred space; you will see how quickly you are able to instill beneficial habits that replace all the contrary ones (that make life miserable). Your spouse is like no one else in the whole world. You are bound to each other in ways that give both of you huge incentives to treat each other wonderfully; you need to treat your spouse wonderfully.

Imagination is the tool of the mind that creates. God handed you a chip off of His Divine block and tells you to have fun. Instead, you use it for rather mundane purposes. That's fine if that is what you choose, but imagination is better used for noble purposes. The more happiness causing uses for imagination are drawing, writing, inventing, and cooking for your spouse. What deadens imagination is staring into a TV or computer monitor for hours on end. For you and your spouse the greatest use of imagination is enhancing your mutual admiration and expressions of love and support.

The Subconscious Mind

The subconscious mind is the reservoir of all your memories, experiences, philosophies and everything that has ever taken place in your life. The subconscious doesn't do any computing at all; creativity and calculation takes place in the conscious mind. Whatever goes into the subconscious is there in the form it was put; storing without comment. The subconscious mind stores both right and wrong conclusions (it has no discrimination); your conscious mind uses stored information without checking it for accuracy. If a person grows up in a household where racial prejudice is accepted, for instance, that person will have prejudicial beliefs without ever having thought about it, until they have some reason to question the wisdom of their prejudice. That is why it is a good practice to reevaluate your conclusions based on fresh evaluations.

If your spouse does something you have labeled *evil*, you will automatically be repulsed, unless you retrain your reactions and stop the mind. You are in charge of your mind and can reject the old habit of thoughts and feelings that reduce you, even from the subconscious. As you correct your thoughts and behaviors one at a time, you automatically change the reservoir of information in your subconscious mind for the better. At the same time, when your spouse errs by reflecting the misinformation in their subconscious and you control your automatic reaction, you give them a chance to correct their thoughts and feelings (if they want to). However, if you react, which forces them to react, you become engaged in an automatic (always meaningless) war; both of you will miss an excellent opportunity to temper your views with love from the upper mind and wisdom.

The process of cleansing the subconscious mind must remain your assignment for the rest of your life. The results of your efforts, however, are immediate and continue as long as you continue to make the effort. I repeat: the pain of the effort required to get out of suffering is far less than the pain of suffering.

You are a good person; you may have detrimental thoughts. Everyone does at times. You are not your thoughts. Even if you act on some of them from time to time, you merely slipped. Though you will pay for your slip, you have not become evil.

There is no question that there is suffering in this world. Your marriage is a safe harbor from worldly suffering when you treat your spouse with loving respect. The effort exerted toward gaining freedom from long-entrenched habits is well worth the slight discomfort it may cause.

The gate of your mind is a good place to start regaining control. When a thought or feeling comes that is beneficial (because it makes you happy or serves someone) you should invite it in and invite its brothers and sisters, aunts, and uncles—all its friends. Make the good thoughts feel welcome and nourished; make the good feelings feel right at home. Then there are the "bad" ones. You know what I'm talking about—nasty, mean, selfish, and critical thoughts (just to characterize a few). These guys are evil,

The pain of the effort required to get out of suffering is far less than the pain of suffering.

and you must prevent their access no matter how much they try to convince you they belong—they don't! They wear disguises such as *fairness, reasonableness, justice.* (Would you demand the same justice for your child or try forgiveness instead?) They work on convincing you they belong and you need them. Man the gates! Don't let them in... No problem, right? Ha! We both know these thoughts get in and ruin your day, almost no matter how hard you try. It is unwelcome thoughts and feelings that ruin your fun—not your spouse. Remember, you cannot control your spouse; but you can control, with practice, your thoughts and feelings. Over time, you get stronger and win more often. The trick is always try to control your thoughts and feelings; **never ever give up**.

Initially use your eviction powers. Your mental sentries have been on vacation and need time to regain control of the gates to your mind; they will. In the meantime, as you realize that these bad guys have been partying in your mind at your expense, you have to kick them out. Do it! Use your wisdom-guided will power and fight them till you win. Honest to God, it's not easy sometimes, but it's a hell of a lot easier to fight them than allow evil thoughts and feelings to take up residence.

The suffering you go through when you don't make the effort is tremendous. Your whole future will improve with a little effort now.

Satan's Soldiers
(This is only metaphorical)

By thinking of harmful thoughts and feelings as evil entities, it is easier to identify and thus defeat them.

- Fear
- Worry
- Anger
- Doubt
- Lust
- Envy
- Selfishness
- Greed
- Impatience

- Prejudice
- Cliquishness
- Superiority
- Inferiority
- Moodiness
- Depression
- Vengefulness
- Loneliness
- Addictions

You can add to the list!

Once these parasites are in, they can be difficult to evict. Eviction requires your good soldiers of *will power* and *discriminative wisdom* guided by the speaking voice of a silent God—*conscience*.

The soldiers of righteousness are few, but they are more powerful. The more you correct your mind the greater your ability becomes. Unless you reduce your will power with drugs, alcohol, or other underminers, you will win the war, even if you lose some of the battles.

Fear is the grand sire of almost all your troubles. Think about it. If you add fear to the knowledge of not getting something you want, you get angry. Add the fear of getting hurt to ordinary caution and you become panicked. Add fear to temporary shortage and greed jumps in. Fear is crafty. Fear comes in the guise of your savior. After all, self-preservation is the body's number-one concern, and fear tells you that this or that will end your life. Its mission is to get you to jump into fight or flight. It does not want you to use reason or discrimination because calm consideration takes energy away from an emergency reaction. Do you see how this works? Caution is not evil, but it gets replaced by fear through misapplication of imagination. Caution is completely reasonable, but when you stop evaluating the cautionary signals (out of habit) with wisdom and reason fear jumps in!

Fear has dominion over a lazy or weak (disease, drugs, exhaustion and alcohol) mind. The best and only way to defeat fear is to face it. Tell your mind you will not follow the fight-or-flight path; you will evaluate your situation dispassionately, ignoring thoughts and feelings springing from fear until you have a workable solution—that's it! The alternative to facing fear is succumbing to it. When you succumb to fear, you get weaker. Therefore, the more often you succumb, the smaller will be the fear that you will succumb to in the future. Eventually you are a mess, unable to stand up for yourself against these destructive thoughts and feelings. Some people use alcohol, medication, or even drugs to get through the hard spots. Hard spots are opportunities to strengthen your will and sharpen your skills. Running from fear is like throwing gasoline on a fire—highly destructive.

The Futility of Worry

During the Great Depression, a businessman in New York City found his company in danger of going under. Due to the upset economy, money was tight and his sales were off. He worked tirelessly to find a solution to his dilemma. Nevertheless, after all his calculations it looked as though he was going to have a huge shortfall and there was no source from which to borrow more money. He was nearly exhausted from all his effort, so he went for a walk in Central Park just to let his brain relax for a few minutes before he hit the books again.

He sat on a park bench after a nice walk when a well-dressed elderly gentleman came by and asked if it was all right to sit with him. He said it was fine and barely took note of the gentleman as his mind was still preoccupied with his business problems. After some time the elderly gentleman mentioned he looked worried and offered to hear his problems, just as a sounding board. The grateful man poured his heart out and felt much better after doing so. Sometimes sharing a problem without asking for help is very beneficial.

After a few questions, the gentleman introduced himself as J. D. Rockefeller, took out his checkbook, and wrote a check for one million dollars. He said all he asked was that they meet in one year at the same bench. If he needed the money, he agreed to pay him back with interest. The man got up, thanked his new benefactor, and went off to work.

A year later, the man went back to the park and sure enough Mr. Rockefeller was sitting on the bench. The man gleefully handed the check he had taken a year before and told Mr. Rockefeller the security of the check was enough; he never had to cash it. Just then a nurse approached. Smiling, she said, "I hope you haven't been bothered sir. Our dear friend likes to tell people he is J. D. Rockefeller."

You have much more security when you put your faith in God. It is always a good idea to pray.

Visualize worry as a dark demon that keeps whispering negative scenarios into your consciousness, keeping your mind occupied on events that never even take place. When you worry about something, it never happens. If you know something is going to happen (that threatens), you can always do something to avoid the catastrophe. Worry is not there to help you; it is there to take your mind off the beauty that is all around you as well as possible solutions to your problems. Like fear, it is not your friend. It is fear's sibling; tell it to get lost! Replace doubt and fear with an expectation that everything is going to work out even though you may not momentarily see how.

The Keys

1. Watch your thoughts and feelings.

2. Toss out the thoughts and feelings that are not absolutely positive in nature.

3. Fill your mind with thoughts and feelings that are strictly positive and beneficial.

   Step one—recognize your mind's bad habits and list them.

   Step two—prioritize your unwanted habits worst first.

   Step three—devise an effective strategy to replace unwanted habits.

   Step four—monitor your progress daily.

A powerful method for changing habit traits is to replace the ones you do not like with their opposite positive trait.

Replace:

- Nervousness with calmness
- Sadness with happiness
- Anger with understanding
- Meanness with sweetness
- and so on

Write down a number of examples of how you can express these opposite traits. The goal is to instill in your mind new desirable habits whenever conditions stimulate the undesirable bad habit.

The night I completed this chapter I followed the advice and looked for my worst habit. As soon as I locked on to it, my mind began to come up with excuses for the unwanted behavior; it was typical. I laughed at the tenacity of the survival instinct to *protect* me. I brushed off the excuses and instructed my mind on how to behave when the habit popped up.

The next day I bumped into someone who had read an early version of my manuscript and was still having critical thoughts about her husband (who she loves dearly). Because she asked me for a strategy, I suggested that every time she had a negative thought, she drop what she was doing and call her husband with some words of praise. I told her to start right now and do it without fail for three days. I assured her the mind will be retrained by then but she should remain vigilant for a week. Sometimes the mind will convince you the habit is changed when it is merely hiding the tendency till you stop hunting it. Don't be fooled! Just go after one bad habit at a time; you will be successful. Go after the ones that negatively impact your spouse.

Conscience: The Speaking Voice of a Silent God

One day after a rain, my then three-year-old daughter and I were out walking, looking for mud puddles to play in. Some psychologist (the same one who told me God is an abstract thought) told her there was no God, so it was my job to tell her the truth. It was a beautiful, windy day. We were barefoot (searching out mud puddles is a serious endeavor and one must be prepared). I said, "I can't see the wind," and she repeated it. (Isn't it so cute how three-year-old girls do that?) I then said, "I can't touch the wind," and she repeated it. Finally, I said, "I can feel the wind, so I know it's there." She repeated that too.

Then I said, "I can't see God," and she repeated it. Then I said, "I can't touch God," and she repeated it. Finally, I said, "I can feel love, so I know He's there," and she repeated that too. Three-year-olds understand God as love because their minds are not overwhelmed with mundane trivialities; they trust their feelings, unclouded by worries that come from the psychophysiological imperatives of self-preservation and procreation.

Your Conscience

You already know your conscience whispers to you whenever you are open to it. The trick is to keep listening. God's advice is perfect. Think of how often you ignored what you heard and how much suffering you had to endure. When we listen to our conscience, it speaks to us more loudly. When we ignore it, the voice becomes almost inaudible as we drown out the wisdom with emotional desires and bad habits. The best way to utilize your precious friend is to note the advice when it is coming to you. Then, test the advice in your mind by imagining possible outcomes, pros and cons.

Sometimes we are unable to muster the required strength to follow the guidance of our conscience; I know that. Therefore, I will pass on advice given me from a dear friend: "If you gotta go into the bar and have a drink, bring God with you." (It is metaphorical.) Never imagine for a second that God is judging and condemning you. God loves you. He is the ultimate mother and father. I must share what I once heard in a spiritual lecture:

If you gotta go into the bar and have a drink, bring God with you

Imagine a mommy watching her baby grab on to the couch and slowly struggle to pull herself up for the very first time. Imagine the toothless smile as the baby realizes the accomplishment, supported by the beaming, proud mommy. What a blissful moment. Then the baby inevitably falls. Mommy says, "Oh my wonderful child; I am so proud of you! You did it!" Right? Of course! Can you ever imagine a mommy saying anything along the lines of, "You stupid loser; you should have taken your first step while you were up there!" Of course not! Mothers and fathers support each step of a child's progress and always downplay setbacks. Parents know effort brings success after failures; that is the usual course. Experience brings mistakes and mistakes bring wisdom. God created us and loves us more than we are able to imagine. When we seem to fail in our own eyes, it is seen by God the same way we see our child take the first missteps of life; God is happy for our progress and never judges our failed attempts. He only asks us to never give up. I find it interesting that most Eastern religions regard shame and guilt as sins.

Imagination

The more you exercise your will power and imagination, the stronger these two tools become. Although there are no gauges that measure strength of will and imagination, we are all cognizant when we encounter people with strong or weak will and/or imagination. You can control these tools and strengthen them if you want. Through disuse, they weaken. Through conscious use, they strengthen.

If you replace negative thoughts and feelings with positive ones, you will be happy; it is that simple and not as difficult as you may imagine. When imagination runs on autopilot in the untrained and undisciplined mind, it exaggerates negative situations; fear and grief overcomes you before you realize what is happening. Imagine watching a movie where cracks form in the Hoover Dam and spread quickly into a nightmarish chain of devastating events. If soon afterward you went to Hoover Dam, your memory would recall the scene with your imagination feeding off what you just saw. The frightening scene would reconstruct in your mind and suggest danger. I can't remember how long it took me to get back in the ocean after watching *Jaws*, but the fear stayed with me a long time; such is the power imagination has over us. This process is perfectly capable of taking off into stratospheric proportions if not under your control. The only one who has the ability to prevent this process from ruining your day is you.

Imagine your spouse telling you she or he bumped into an old friend of the opposite sex—uh oh! Your mind would probably find something to worry about because of past bad habits of suspicion and jealousy weighing heavily against your actual knowledge. Your imagination may lead you down a path of jealousy, fear, or anger by imagining all sorts of possibilities that drive you crazy. Perhaps it will convince you (notice I said *it*) the meeting was pre-arranged, or perhaps more than casual, or God knows what.

The imagination left to the influences of untrained habits opens the door to a whole series of thoughts, which do much harm to your marriage. The alternative is to control the mind, reign in your imagination from its misguided roll of evil provocateur, and *redirect it* to beneficial thoughts, feelings, and behavior. You can redirect to thoughts of compassion for the old friend and true concern for how the meeting might have affected your spouse. Imagination may come up with a zillion plausible scenarios and back them up with all kinds of preposterous rationales just to keep you engaged. It is doing its job. Don't get sucked in!

When it comes to your spouse, *always* assume the best. Never buy in to derogatory thoughts. When attacked by thoughts of suspicion, it is not okay to share with your spouse in a way that defines the problem as some allegation that forces your spouse to get defensive; that is not nice! It is very intimidating to be accused. Rather than retaliating for behavior you suspect may be taking place, use all your power to win your spouse's love and affection through ideal behavior. Even if your suspicions prove true, nothing good will come from confrontation. Let the past be past. Always behave as well as you can.

If you are an ideal spouse, you will never have to fear unfaithfulness. Many individuals have said they should not have to worry about the integrity of their spouse. I say, "Right, don't!" Worry about your own—are you living up to the promises you made? Usually the cost of forgiveness is very low compared with the future benefits. Until you are perfect, it is a good idea to focus on your own flaws. Your imagination greatly exaggerates most marital problems. You expect perfection of your spouse but not yourself. When I have read back some "marriage buster" problems to some of my clients and reframed them without the traditional emotional components, they did all they could to not burst out laughing. That is not to say all problems are minimal, but they will all reduce in impact by *proper* use of imagination. Make your imagination a positive, instead of negative, tool of the mind.

Free Choice

Most of us actually believe we have complete free choice. That would be wonderful if it were true; every time something came up you would weigh the pros and cons. Imagine sitting on a throne where you dispassionately judge a situation based on lofty principles with no fears or worries, creating long-term beneficial outcomes for all involved. How many times have you judged the decision of an authority, noting how they succumbed to some external pressure?

You may forget that everyone is pressured by habits, prejudice, and personal survival drives. Unfortunately, they gave up free choice a long time ago, just like you, and have become a victim of those limitations without ever knowing it. Is it not ironic to get upset when anyone tries to impose on our free choice when we have pretty much thrown it away anyway? If you start your car, aim it, put it in gear, step on the gas, and take your hands off the steering wheel, you will be in big trouble. The body/mind is your vehicle; you must take control.

The mind is not mysterious. It's yours; control it!

The mind's functions are understandable. It's yours; control it!

The mind is controllable. It's yours; control it!

Most people will tell a child to control himself. I tell children to control their *minds*. This is not semantics or splitting hairs. Children (and you) have minds that need to be understood and controlled—teach them; it isn't too late. If your child feels fear, tell her to ignore it and proceed cautiously. If he feels anger, tell him to push that anger out of his mind as fast as he can and shift his perspective and feel sympathy for the person he is mad at. If she feels sad, tell her to pull in thoughts that bring her happiness. There is no challenge they cannot overcome; they should never be a victim of some errant thought or feeling. It is their mind and they must control it or it will control them! Your children need your guidance. Feel free to share your wisdom with them so that they learn while they are young.

Will Power

Use Your Will Intentionally

You have the supreme weapon for conquering psychological enemies: will power. Use your will power intentionally; free will is meaningless without the determination to do what you choose *because* you choose. It is easy to give in to your habitual wrong desires—don't! Use your will to control your mind; behave admirably. Free choice is yours only when you make the effort. Like a muscle, will is strengthened by use and atrophies through disuse; it is also weakened by drugs, alcohol, bad health, poor diet, and a desultory life.

It is better to act incorrectly (still doing your best) with will, than not to act at all. Just be sure your actions are controlled.

The more you do with specific intention the more actual control you have over future events of your life. Don't leave things to chance. Just as you are reading these lessons (an act of intentional will) to improve your marriage, so you can change everything by doing your best to improve your circumstances. If you don't take control of your mind, who will?

What you *can* control (or have power to control) are

1. Thoughts and feelings you allow into your mind (the first thought is not controllable; the next ones are)

2. Thoughts and feelings you keep in your mind

3. What you do with those thoughts and feelings (Do you get depressed, excited, angry?)

4. How you interpret communications (Do you take everything personally?)

5. What you say, including your response to others

6. How you behave

7. How much you smile and frown

8. Your moods (Honest! You are in charge of your moods.)

In short, you have the power to control your body, thoughts, feelings, and behavior, including emotions and speech.

You absolutely cannot control the above in *anyone* else. Respect your spouse's free will even if he or she is not respecting you. It is not your place to point out what they should and should not do. Furthermore, your behavior ought not to be dependent upon the behavior of your spouse, boss, or some mean bureaucrat. If you act angrily because someone did something mean, you have become a victim of your own behavior, not theirs.

Do what you should do, not what you (the habit bound mind) want to do

Will power is your strongest psychological soldier

Getting revenge is like taking poison and waiting for your enemy to die. Go one step further; stop desiring certain behavioral changes. Accept your spouse's imperfections. **Appreciate your spouse for who she or he is.** Your relationship will change instantly because you have changed your own expectations and behavior. This is the key to happiness; change yourself into a happy person. Outer circumstances are what they are. Blaming externals for how you are feeling is folly. Don't be a victim of life's challenges. Make happy and beneficial thoughts fill your mental environment. Temporary pleasures, big and small, do not combine to create happiness. Don't be a sucker by striving for little happy moments when you can be happy all the time by controlling your thoughts.

Happiness will appear instantly to those who shift their perspective. Blame is a loser's game no matter what; happiness is your own responsibility. I know it seems easier to go along with old habits even though you know they don't work. You will need to expend effort. Happily, even the smallest amount of sincere effort will yield great results. The more effort you make, the happier you will be. Most people wait for the other shoe to drop because they have been self-trained to suffer. Screw that! **You don't have to suffer anymore. You don't have to fear anything anymore.**

Behavior Modification Versus Personality Change

Change comes in two distinct forms. The lesser form is behavior modification; the superior is personality or character change. Changing yourself correctly requires changing current seemingly innate qualities that guide your choices. Some people actually believe this kind of major change is as impossible as changing your DNA—it ain't!

Be patient with your own flaws as well as your spouse's flaws

Nobody can force or inspire someone to change. Change comes when it is the obvious thing to do from the person's point of view, usually because their habitual traits are causing too much pain too often. Don't impose your expectations on others. Focus on your needs for beneficial self change. Remember, personal growth is just that—personal. You are neither a teacher nor a student of your spouse. Be supportive when your spouse is tackling a flaw the way you would be if you were watching a fireman go into a burning building to rescue a child. Stand back; don't get in the way, but be super supportive. On the other hand, when you are the fireman, recognize that your supporters may sometimes go too far. Accept their unwanted help for what it is and just ignore most of it with a smile. Don't get mad, they mean well. The only one "outside" of you who can help you is God. (Him you can ask for help. Him you *should* ask for help!)

Behavior modification is like training a kitty to not attack the birdie you put on her head. After the compelling inducement of your total attention no longer controls the kitty's instincts, the sweet kitty becomes a cat again; birdie is lunch. Behavior modification means control of your natural inclinations. In order to accommodate your better judgment, you modify your behavior on a temporary basis. It's not how you would "want" to act, but you modify your behavior to be appropriate for the situation.

In a dispute with a motor vehicle department employee, for instance, after standing in line for half an hour, the clerk you see says you were in the wrong line and no one in charge will allow you to get in front of the correct line. Everything in you wants to either scream or pull out all stops and explain in a loud voice what you think about their systems. Instead of blasting away, however, you decide it would only make matters much worse if you spoke up. So you put on a pleasant face, bite your tongue, and proceed to the correct line (nice kitty).

You modified your behavior because your personality or character (being un-Gandhi-like) would have had you behaving in a universally destructive way. Think about the cat trained to let the parakeet sit on its head. As long as someone is reminding the cat how it must behave, everything is fine. However, if you don't force the behavior as time passes, the natural instincts of the cat will make the bird a plaything and snack. The cat will never think it did anything wrong. The cat's character was not changed merely by repetition or training. If, however, you could convince the cat that it is a dog, the bird will be safe. Dogs have different personality traits, and they don't have a value system that identifies birds as snacks. Similarly, a person's character will not change because of mere repetition or reward/punishment training.

A person, blessed with free will, can change his or her values, principles, and perspectives, literally becoming a different type

People resist change when they are asked to change by others

Be very patient with others— especially your spouse

of person. We can overcome long-embedded bad habits. You can replace them with beneficial ones. Personality flaws that produce undesirable results in one situation will produce undesirable results in countless situations. In the case of the motor vehicle department, if you got upset and you will get upset anytime you feel you are treated unfairly. You will feel successful when you modify your behavior, but you are still stuck with the resulting tensions caused by not being able to do what you felt you wanted to do. This is like jumping in a lake without knowing how to swim, sinking to the bottom and running until you get to the shore. People go through life intermittently controlling themselves, believing they have been successful because they adapted to a situation in a way that kept them out of more trouble until one fine day they question why they always find themselves in these situations. They realize blaming the world has done nothing to help ease the painful results. They understand that the world is what it is; and it ain't gonna change. When it is clear the world won't conform to them they find a way to live more harmoniously.

On that proverbial day (the light must go on many times before it remains on), the individual decides something on the inside must change. They realize behavior modification (though not previously called that) is a quick-fix band-aid that only masks the pain. They realize they have to become a different person; a person who does not get affected so easily, a person who takes more in stride. Then they begin changing their character or personality by stopping the mental reaction and telling their mind that what just happened was not a big deal. They tell themselves they are better than that, more mature and evolved; and they force their minds into a peaceful state more conducive to happiness. Over time, the individual becomes less sensitive and more like the kind of person they choose to be; they commit to letting go of old habits.

Simply put, you have the ability to change the person you are into one who is more loving and tolerant. The person you married mirrors both your good and bad quality traits which helps you see your weaknesses (and strengths) more clearly. The mere effort toward change will bring very good feelings, while resistance to the outer warnings will increase your suffering. You might conclude that God set up a natural reward/punishment system designed to help

You have the ability to change the person you are.

Our obligatory role in a relationship is to be supportive—not critical.

120

you evolve without anyone actually pointing out your flaws. When you control your mind and subdue its passions, you are rewarded with happiness. When you act as if the world must conform to your desires, you will suffer. This cosmic law is rock hard like gravity. It is wise to recognize this law and use it to your advantage. It is dumb to keep banging your head against the wall of desires for control of the world around you. Control your own mind. The tools to create change, as previously conveyed, are *wisdom*, *reason*, and *will power*. You can do it!

Our obligatory role in a relationship is to be supportive—not critical. Being complimentary when we are not feeling complimentary produces good results for all. When your mind is negative and you force it to go down a positive path, you are gaining control over it. Like weight lifting, exercising your muscles gives you power and control. The more you exercise, the more capable you become and the greater your successes. Be patient in the beginning. But remember you are only to work on your own flaws. When you become aware of a flaw in your spouse quickly jump to a positive trait and point it out to your spouse with all the enthusiasm you can muster. Be their greatest fan club.

Keep up the effort. Curb your negative thoughts and expectations until you have become perfect. Practice replacing disruptive thought and feelings with pleasant thoughts and feelings. You will notice immediate results.

We must work toward changing ourselves and not each other. It is a grave error to try to critique and fix your spouse. They will not be receptive and you will miss an opportunity to tend to your own flaws. A gracious spouse will sometimes pretend to be grateful when you point out their flaws, but they can't do much with that kind of feedback. If your spouse asks for critiquing, it is imperative you politely decline for both your sakes. If you notice growth in your spouse, it is probably okay to compliment the newly acquired trait without pointing out the newness of it. You might say, "I love how complimentary you are" instead of, "Gee honey, you have become much sweeter. Thank God." **The only people you may actively help in their pursuit of personal growth are your children. It is an obligation to help them with their personal growth.**

If something bugs you, it is your problem and you need to get debugged; you are too hard to please, anyway. When you pipe in

The commonly accepted idea that couples help each other grow is false and dangerous.

Focus on your spouse's positive qualities

with *constructive* criticism, the best you can hope for is neutral acceptance; the potential for a misunderstanding is very high. **If you respond to criticism with a sincere compliment, the only way the conversation can go is up.** More than one person has sincerely told me that they are easy-going except with their spouse. They had not yet understood that the people we are closest to test our limits of patience, compassion, etc. It isn't their fault; it is just not easy to avoid blemishes when we are in tight quarters. All our weaknesses come to the fore.

I know psychologists mean something else when they talk about the inner child, but this definition is more on the money. Your inner child is the *mind*. It has been unregulated for so long and needs some loving discipline. It's crying, "Please teach me to behave. Don't listen to my tantrums and excuses. Love me by guiding me to be good." Some traits may take years to change. Don't worry. If you keep at it, you can remove even the most pernicious mental enemies. Your effort alone will bring great results. Complete success is not immediately important. The effort is what pays off rather than reaching perfection. You and your spouse married each other knowing that you each had flaws both big and little. You knew you did have and still have flaws. Don't worry about them. If one of eighty-eight keys on a piano is not working, you don't throw out the piano! Stop being so hard on yourself and each other.

I worked with one couple whose female half is very likely clinically depressed. I am not a psychologist, so I never test anyone or really put much stock in the supposed value of knowing psychological profiles. However, in her case it was obvious she was not capable of following the above suggestions of controlling her mind. This was obvious to anyone, and her dear husband was beside himself because the psychologists they met with suggested splitting up, years of therapy for both, and getting meds for her. If there were no children, they never would have come to me; but he was desperate to endure whatever he needed to for the sake of his children. She, too, would do anything for their kids.

She wanted no part of meds (I have no idea if that is a good or bad thing) and so he was, in his own mind, stuck. I took them through the whole process. They seemed to retain it, but he called me and told me that she was not following through. I met with him in private and explained that if he saw her behavior as a disease and himself as a supportive friend it might give him a different perspective. He needed to not take her behavior personally. After several weeks, he called me again and told me that he never felt so much peace because the technique of reframed detachment allowed him to disengage from the drama. He said he now played the role of an observer of himself when situations popped up and he watched his own mind react. Then he would coax it back into a neutral position. He stopped engaging in her drama and stopped taking her symptomatic outbursts personally.

Though his wife was not making any apparent progress, he was able to be there for her more. I predict the pressure will continue to fall away for both of them. In the meantime, their kids are safe and he is growing in ways he never imagined. When she is ready, she will tackle her own mental enemies in the way that she chooses, or not. The marriage is safe now because she does not feel threatened by his reactions and he feels like he is there for her and their children. Though not ideal, it is beautiful and lovely. We are not the judges of what is working and not working for others. He is happy in the marriage because he loves his wife and kids and has a chance to demonstrate his love and add value to all their lives. She is struggling but protected and would not struggle any less out of the relationship. The kids have both parents under one roof where service to each other overrides selfishness—looks pretty good to me!

Imagine you were eating some candy that you discovered in the cupboard. Then someone came along and told you conclusively that the candy was laced with tiny amounts of arsenic meant for killing rodents. You would simply cease eating the candy. The habit of reaching for some may keep you reaching a couple of times, but the new habit of recalling the poison will take over very soon. Well, your non-harmony producing behavior, no matter how sweet it may seem by the standards of *justified* reactions, is self-poisoning. The bad habit of being mean will soon give way to remembrance that it is poison and you will replace the bad habit with the sweetness-producing habits of loving behavior. Watch your thoughts and control your mind. Habits can be good or bad.

Most people make the mistake of thinking that their happiness depends on how they are treated. This is completely false. Though one may have some temporary feelings of gratification from an external occurrence, happiness comes from within.

If you choose to be happy, nothing and no one can make you unhappy; and if you choose to be unhappy, nothing and no one can make you happy.

Don't put off your happiness! If you switch partners, it's only a matter of time before you bring back all the same conditions that plague you now. It is your behavior that needs to be changed. If you fertilize the most durable plant in the world with gasoline, it will die. Your marriage requires the fertilizer of respect, consideration, and kindness to prosper. It does not need the poisons most of you have been giving it.

A few of you are still thinking it's not you, it's your spouse. So, in other words, you are perfect? Or maybe your spouse is more of the problem than you? Trust me; your spouse thinks the same thing. It makes no difference how he or she behaves if you make up your mind to work on you and that's all you concern yourself with. You can define your happiness, but you can never control your environment.

Even if your spouse will not read this or listen to this, your marriage will still work. (If you try to talk about it, they will possibly see it as an attack; and they will probably be right.). Life is not fair and neither are angry spouses. So you just work on yourself and be the best spouse you can be.

Pray. Ask for His help that you can get control over your mind and learn to live a joyous and harmonious marital existence by following His rules for happiness.

I promise you that if you stop criticizing your spouse and concentrate your effort on behaving like an amazing spouse yourself, you will be happy no matter what your spouse does. I promise!

As I wrote this book, I sometimes asked for comments from various people just to get an idea of how what I wrote was taken. I wanted to make sure it came out as I meant it—especially the more complex thoughts. One man who read the paragraph about being happy no matter what your spouse does emphatically said that he disagreed. He told me that when he was married, he walked into his home to find his wife with his best friend. He said, "No matter what kind of husband I was, there she was."

It wasn't like I was going to go there with him. The poor guy really suffered and he was not in a place to hear what he would have perceived as a lecture (one must always be sensitive to another's state of mind). But the fact is the logic still stands. He is not responsible for his wife's betrayal; and though he probably took some measure of responsibility for what she did, the truth is that he can only be responsible for what he does. Suffering is part of living and we get plenty of opportunity to suffer. We also have the opportunity to mitigate our own suffering by controlling our mind and behavior. Because that is the limit of our control, we should take full advantage of it and not waste our energy trying to change that which we cannot. Everyone has unlimited potential for perennial joy and happiness. Become a fountain of goodness and you will never doubt again.

Your To Do List

1   Pray for your spouse's happiness and ask for guidance on how you can be a better spouse.

2   Demand of your self that you will cease all non-positive expressions.

3   Create a plan for eliminating your worst habit by replacing it with the opposite good habit.

Loyalty—The Highest Law

*E*xcept for blatant con-artists, everyone thinks of themselves as loyal. That is good because everyone should be loyal. The problem is the tests of loyalty have gotten too easy to pass, and our ability to rationalize away this most important quality is taught daily by Hollywood's version of right and wrong—TV soap operas, comedies, and movies as well as magazines all look for and focus on rationalizing. Our schools do not teach us grounded morality or life skills because we have gone too far in the separation of *church and state* (excluding God as well as religion), and we certainly do not have many worthy role models in our society. In fact, the idea of what *loyal* means is very fluid in our society, and most people are naturally confused. You, as a married person, should not be confused because loyalty is very important. Although a breech in loyalty is not the end of the world and is usually recoverable, it can be very difficult for the betrayed.

Infidelity is the disloyalty we will address first. There is no real excuse for infidelity (the most destructive form of marital disloyalty), and I never slight the seriousness of this type of behavior. On the other hand, the right way to deal with this is to make it an event that will not destroy your marriage and your children's lives. I address this one problem in particular because we are fighting against cultural standards that on the one hand almost give permission for infidelity (in some cases) yet ironically tell us it makes marriage unrecoverable (though it is far from fatal most of the time). For the sake of your children, it is of critical importance to overcome this challenge if you have been betrayed. I will enroll you as a saint!

Loyalty is a grand expression of love

For those who have been betrayed

Those who stray do so because they do not feel loved and appreciated. Please do not judge this description of their sense of what is *missing* for them or become defensive by saying there is no excuse (which I agree with) if you are the victim of betrayal. I am merely stating a fact. Even those who, "got drunk and didn't know what they were doing when a prostitute came to their hotel room by mistake" did not feel loved and appreciated. The person who cheats on their spouse is suffering (in their marriage) and is looking for a way to relieve the pain. Without excusing this behavior it is important to understand it. As far as forgiveness goes, I am not asking you to forgive and move on—not yet. I am only asking you to understand why your spouse cheated. Your spouse faced temptation and gave in because of their own weakness; not to hurt you. They will pay a huge price for their misdeeds, but you want to know how to get your marriage back on track. This is a tough one. But the only couple I "lost" happened when I sent the mom (who was having the affair) to a child psychologist for help with her kids. He told her to live her "dream" (that their three- and five-year-old boys would be fine). She traded off her children for her pride! Your marriage can still achieve the sweetness you have always sought even though betrayal occurs. The biggest obstacle to your happiness if you are the betrayed is your anger and, more to the point, humiliation. We will address this. If your spouse doesn't know you know, don't say anything.

Leave the past to the past

If you are a cheater

I have some advice for you: First, put your children ahead of your own needs. These kids are God's, and you are entrusted with raising them to the best of your ability and then some. If you break up your family just because you are not getting enough sex (men) or you are not getting the right kind of attention (women), you are going to pay a karmic debt that will not go away until it is paid in full. Eastern psychology describes treachery as an unforgivable offense because treachery is always premeditated. This means that you will pay the full karmic debt—so hang on to your shorts. Most karmic payback is eventually effectively reduced through education; and with Divine intervention, penance is reduced (with prayer). The full load, however, must be borne by the treacherous person.

Pray with all your might for forgiveness and don't do it again. If you are in the midst of an affair, cut it off and change your habits so you never have to see the person again. Write a "stay away" letter to your accomplice in crime (avoid all personal or phone contact) and even change jobs if you need to. You are in the jaws of the beast and you are being chewed up without knowing because Satan has duped you into thinking, "this is different." The anesthetic will wear off, though, and the pain will come—this I promise! What you did was you walked away from your life and responsibilities because you didn't like it and chose not to fix it. (Okay, until you read this book you didn't know how, but now you know what to do! God considers that too.) It's like living in an apartment that you never clean, so you go out to eat all the time because your kitchen is too messy.

In some rare cases, it may be unavoidable not to tell your spouse that you cheated, but it is not your duty to do so. The pain of the betrayal is yours, and it will come to you. Do not put some of your pain onto your spouse because that will only bring on more bad karma. If your spouse knows (and this is rare unless you help them find out), you need to accept their reaction as legitimate regardless of how unfair it seems to you (yes, cheaters have so rationalized their behavior that they think they should be *understood* and forgiven—a great example of the survival drive).

If you have read these lessons, you know what it takes to have a great relationship and marriage. Don't think that you can walk away from your spouse and start with someone new with this newfound knowledge; it does not work that way. You have lessons to learn in cleaning up what you have. You need to gather your strength and face your demons. I promise you that Divine help is always there and you will make it if you don't give up. My experience with numerous couples who faced this challenge is that they were always successful and had a great marriage. Ignore the statistics caused by the current failures of Western psychology.

Betrayed one, it is not your fault your spouse cheated on you. Interestingly it is usually the most die-hard spouse that ends up with a cheater. If you were an incarnation of perfection, I would first ask you how you ended up with someone who can do this to you. But I know the answer. The doctrines in Eastern psychology explain that man is evolving as an individual. This evolution is instigated by numerous factors, number one of which is suffering—not just any suffering, but tailor-made suffering designed to get your attention and force you to change yourself until eventually you have what God intends for you, a blissful existence. Everyone wants that.

We talk about how crazy the world is and how much evil there is, but the truth is *we* are those crazy and evil aspects of the world that make it as it is. As we evolve into better, kinder people, we contribute to the improvement of the world and its evil affects us less. Our suffering is not meant to hurt us. It is meant to show us our weaknesses and flaws. Think of a child who freaks out because he did not get the candy he wanted just before dinner. His suffering is very real. The parent guides the child to understand it is his attachment to the desire that is causing his suffering, so the child evolves. So it is with our challenges. They set us up to recognize how our suffering comes, not from the behavior of others over whom we have no control, but from our own attachments and flaws. No matter how intense and how out of whack our situation is, or how obviously twisted someone else's behavior toward us is, it is up to us to overcome our suffering by changing ourselves. Naturally, it is also up to us to take practical steps to prevent further problems, but I'm talking about the suffering. I'm talking about using your smarts to reveal a perspective that benefits you and brings you happiness and growth. That which comes to you is yours; there are no mistakes! What you do with what comes to you is where you get to exercise your free will. If betrayal is your lot, I offer my sympathy. I have seen how huge it is. But there are other forms of disloyalty that need to be mentioned.

Dogs are loyal. Cats are not. That's it! Okay, that is not it. In this short chapter, I will be very simple. I will list loyal and disloyal deeds.

Our suffering is not meant to hurt us. It is meant to show us our weaknesses and flaws.

Disloyal deeds

- Thinking bad things about your spouse

- Saying bad things about your spouse

- Flirting with someone else

- Allowing someone to flirt with you for more than four seconds

- Allowing someone to put down your spouse or speak suggestively about them
- Being impolite to your spouse, especially in front of someone else
- Not being supportive of your spouse's ideas
- Putting your own needs ahead of your spouse's
- Checking out other people or thinking about them
- Spending money without agreement
- Keeping kid's secrets from your spouse
- Making plans without your spouse knowing
- Comparing your spouse to others
- Keeping friends who don't like your spouse

- Thinking good things about your spouse
- Saying positive things about your spouse
- Doing small things for your spouse that they like
- Praising your spouse to your kids
- Praising your spouse in general
- Praying for your spouse
- Expanding your love for your spouse
- Helping those in need
- Being kind to your spouse
- Not thinking of your spouse as a sex object
- Not thinking of your spouse as oversexed
- Praying for your spouse's success

Loyal deeds

The above lists are partial, and you may have some great ideas to add. Do not expect loyalty. Expect yourself to be absolutely loyal. If you focus on your own behavior, you will not have time to look at your spouse's behavior, it just takes a shift.

The expression of loyalty is subtle to those whom you are loyal, but only on the surface. Never seek recognition. Loyalty should be given in every relationship. As you develop your loyalty you will feel more and more love because loyalty is an expression of love.

Your relationship will succeed. With what you now know it is up to you to feel the joy of harmony and love. The next and last chapter will seem quite natural to women and a bit awkward for men. That is until you try the techniques of intimacy…Are you ready?...Excellent!

Lesson Twelve

Intimacy

WARNING: If you skipped reading the book, please go back and read it!

espite all my warnings, there are those who will have skipped to this chapter thinking that intimacy and sex are so important to their relationship that if they merely learn the secret to wonderful love making, all else will fall into place. I wish they were right. But it's not so simple. There is much foundational knowledge that you need to grasp before you can have the right frame of mind required for genuine intimacy. This chapter is not about the ultimate orgasm; so if you skipped reading the book, please go back and read it! I am not a sex doctor. What is in this chapter is an accumulation of the right attitudes and perspectives along with scientific understanding so that you can experience a complete, enduring relationship.

The reason there is frustration and confusion around the intimacy aspect of relationships is our Freudian-educated culture doesn't *get it!* Current intimacy theory is very primitive, focusing on the shallowest aspects of sexuality and stimulation. While trying to make sex appear deep and sophisticated, it misses the point that intimacy is supposed to be a seamless part of the relationship as a whole. True connecting requires a combining of the psychological and spiritual sides of you, as well as the physical. It must take place every minute of every day which encompasses intimate lovemaking.

Sexuality was created by God; and although old-time religionists have viewed sex as a loaded gun of sorts, it is only due to misunderstanding. Evolution of humans has changed the way much is viewed, and many taboos must be understood to be appreciated. Authoritarian dictates are meant for little children; the rest of us need reasonable explanations. Although sex is very powerful, it is not bad or evil. Like anything else, even an automobile, you can cause trouble and problems through misuse. The ideological notion that there is something wrong with sex is inaccurate. The psychophysiological imperative to procreate initiates and drives the desire to have sex and was invented by God. It is essential for the continuation of our species and is so ingrained in the body that it creates what seems to be an absolute need, just as the psychophysiological imperative for survival initiates and drives the desire to eat. Whereas the natural drive for food is not considered immoral, it is unfortunate that for many the drive for sex is seen as *bad*. In truth, it is *good* (or at least neutral) and only needs to be understood so that it will further your love and connection. Of course just because it is a natural force does not mean one should just *go with it*. Marriage is not the environment for such recklessness, as some may have thought when they got married. The procreative force needs to be understood and *managed* as best as can be (though not suppressed).

In men this invisible procreative force produces a 24/7 drive for sex

In a man this invisible procreative force produces a 24/7 drive for sex. Man's body tells him his job is to impregnate women. His body tells him to test everything in sight, but remember that only the most barbaric individuals are so undisciplined, out of control, or reckless that this signal is unfiltered and uncontrolled. I am merely making the point that this drive is at the core of man's *lust*. I am not building a case to excuse lustful behavior or objectifying women in any way.

In women the procreative drive has a much more complex manifestation

In a woman the procreative drive has a much more complex manifestation including, but not limited to, bodily and psychological responses to a man's (any man's) bodily desires; initial responses of attraction or repulsion are part of the woman's selection instinct (which is an integral part of what prompts her desire for a certain mate). Regardless of how it manifests distinctively in men and women, this core force is rooted in the same place. Lust is the raw psychological translation of the body's message to procreate. It is not wrong —it just *is*.

An individual can rise above (transcend) lust when they know how. But I am not going to ask you to do that. Instead, I will offer methods for redirecting this powerful energy in ways that will make your lovemaking more connected to your psychological and spiritual sides, thus giving you a deeper and more fulfilling experience.

Lust is primarily the raw form of the drive as expressed without cultural or individual filters. It is usually a masculine condition because of the relative simplicity of nature's expectation of the male, which is to impregnate. The female body is driving her too. But obviously nature has a different plan for how the female responds to her physical drives. Women must carry, nurture, and protect a *new* human being, not only for the first nine months of its existence on Earth but for years afterward. Because the biological requirements of a child are so complex and all consuming, women "require" the aid of a constant male companion and helpmate. Bear in mind that our culture has tremendously altered what used to be a biological need. In our culture, there are choices and children; men and women have all benefited from the flexibility that now exists. But biologically a woman's allure is designed (and intended by nature) to *hold* her man in a supportive role. The co-beneficial synergistic relationship between men and women begins right here. It falls apart if wives unfairly begrudge their husbands for having such an all-consuming drive to have sex or if men think their wives are cold and unsympathetic to their needs.

Women cannot sympathize with their husbands because they do not receive the same bodily messages, so they blame their husband's "warped mind" or just *accept* that this is how he is. Because women do not have similar feelings, they imagine that there are men who do not have such drives. On the other hand, men are bombarded with messages that sexy women who can't wait to have sex are to be found everywhere but home. Both of these false perspectives need to be cleared from your mind. We need to look at how we make things work for both of you instead of lamenting that nature created a lose-lose setup. Could you imagine how difficult procreation would be if men and women had the same sort of drive and it manifested the same way? Women have egg production and viability as the primary triggering mechanism for sexual desire. When the egg is *ready*, the body wants the egg to be fertilized. Because this occurs only once a month for a few hours it would be very tricky to attract a male if he wasn't *ready* all the time. What if the man said, "Sorry honey, I'm just not in the mood." The fact that men are always in the mood is a critical component in the procreation plan. God didn't create all this so we would

God's plan for intimacy works

suffer in our own male/female ways. It would appear as if there is an insurmountable dilemma built into the system. But it is only a dilemma because we do not include our spiritual and psychological nature when we are intimate with our spouse.

God created a plan that directs us toward a balanced approach that encompasses our triune nature of the physical, psychological, and spiritual. He has set it all up so our greatest happiness comes when we work in harmony with His plan. Ladies, it is time to appreciate Mother Nature's design and appreciate your husband's body-driven frustration. Annoyance has never helped. It is not loving or supportive to "put up with it," which is the best that most wives do in our society. And men, it is time to understand why your needs have not been seen as important; women just don't have the drives you do. This is not the end, it is the beginning. I have shared only the basis; and as we go further, you will see how everyone gets more than what they wanted because of how it all works. By lack of understanding, you guys have been driving an airplane on roads wondering what those things (the wings) are there for. I am going to show you how that "airplane" can fly and change your idea of making love forever.

Being focused on an orgasm is very limiting

Current lovemaking for you is probably focused on orgasms; it seems important to have an orgasm. If a man does not have an orgasm, it is often disconcerting, and if the woman doesn't have an orgasm, it doesn't seem fair. Doesn't that tie in with what I stated above? The male orgasm is what is required to make babies, not the holding and caressing, etc. A man's body does not direct him to hold and caress. The animal has just one objective—completion of the sex act for the purpose of procreation. When animals complete the act to serve their body's purpose, they move on and go about their individual business. A woman has a desire for an orgasm because it usually is the best she can hope for out of the deal. She may even self-satisfy to relieve her psychological and physical tension, which seems to take over. In other words, lovemaking is pivoting exclusively around the physical pleasure instead of incorporating activities that stimulate psychological and spiritual fulfillment. Current "proof" of successful lovemaking is an orgasm. Where is the psychological? Where is the spiritual? Some people might say that the psychological needs are also represented in an orgasm, but it isn't intentional and so is "coincidental" at best. By putting all your eggs in the "physical" basket, you are limiting your fulfillment to one third of the potential benefits.

The purpose of marriage is to control procreation and help each other learn to give and receive love. So it stands to reason that the purpose of making love, besides the obvious procreative purpose, is to learn to give and receive love. How? First, I will tell you what is a really bad idea. By making women "horny," we are most of the time going against nature. The woman, let's keep in mind, is not only a wife, but is "designed" to be a mother. And though couples are willing to try almost anything and everything to improve an unhappy marriage, one only needs to ask if they would approve of their daughter going down the path of sexualizing herself. Would you want your daughter to be horny all the time? Honestly, it is tough in our society to avoid this destructive path. The idea of sex as a recreation has taken firm hold and is promoted everywhere, except in homes where there are daughters.

We are *primarily* spiritual beings. We assume we are physical beings, but this is a mistake. We are spiritual beings who have human forms. Most of us agree we have souls, but it is the other way around. We are souls who have bodies. **The highest intimacy is to connect spiritually, soul meeting soul;** we cannot do that when the mind is held by sexual desire. It is important to acknowledge ourselves and our spouse in the highest light possible even if we cannot see it at first. You need to see your spouse through the "eyes" of the heart or the soul. When you look at your spouse's body and desire it with lustful intentions, you are behaving like sophisticated animals. When you wish to join with your spouse from the heart, you begin to rise above our animal nature and being human beings, as God intended.

We know from science that we are condensed "energy" in human form. We know that all matter is actually energy. This energy is not limited to or circumscribed by our physical forms. Individual energy extends beyond your physical form. When you have intercourse, your spiritual energy extends automatically. Women actually feel this without fail and wrongly assume men always feel it too. The trouble is that when our attention is on genitalia, as it usually is during sexual intercourse, our experience is purely physical. That is why we have to ask, "How was it for you?" Being concentrated on the physical causes you to be separated psychologically and

Expand your love making into a physical, spiritual and psychological experience

spiritually. Although your bodies are "connecting," as individuals you are concentrated and focused on your own experience, using your partner's body as a tool for sexual gratification. This is why the orgasm is so important; what else is there? **The answer is to *willfully* shift your intentions and your focus of awareness.**

Although your focus may be on the physical aspects of making love, the reality is there is an exchange of energy taking place anyway. This is super potent and is part of God's plan for helping us open up our heart. It is very deep. When you ignore it, as in recreational sex, you are negatively using your will to block spiritual and psychological awareness. Your most important attribute is love, yet you use your will power to block the awareness of it. In fact, people often use alcohol to obliterate their consciousness in order to numb the effects of missing their birthright. They opt to destroy their own consciousness in order to fulfill the physical drive while pushing away the much more fulfilling psychological and spiritual experience.

Become aware of love. Virtually all people focus on the sensual benefits and effects during intercourse and are barely aware of the ever-present subtle energies. **Put your attention on your heart, *ignore your genitalia* (I promise it will still function).** Project your love to your partner. Use your will and imagination to send waves of love from your heart to theirs. You will experience your partner at a level not yet discovered. By use of will power and imagination you will become better and better at this. There is no end to the heights you will achieve. **When a couple focuses attention on each other during the sexual act there is a commingling of energies. The subtle energies are categorized as spiritual and psychological. The crude energies are physical energies.**

Where we put our attention has everything to do with our experience of making love

One problem some people have in the beginning stages of making intimacy a spiritual experience occurs because man is driven by his *readiness*. I suggest the husband relieve himself through masturbation a few hours prior to meeting his wife. Then the pressure is not overwhelmingly distracting. He can focus better on his wife's heart. (More than one man has suggested his wife help him with this relief. That is a bad idea in the beginning as it is precisely what you want to avoid: making the woman a sex operative.) I also advise wives to be patient. Help your husband by consciously pouring your heart into his. Where we put our attention has everything to do with our experience of making love. If you put your attention on the physical aspects of procreation, as animals do, you become temporarily physically satisfied and then depleted. On the other hand, if you put your attention only on love, which is spiritual, you will experience true intimacy. The spiritual effects last far beyond the effects of physical and psychological release.

Once you understand the principles, it will seem absurd to go backward. Of course "fun sex" is not going to hurt you once in a while as long as you are on track. But the greater experience of what you are learning will speak for itself.

The innate transcendent quality we need to focus on, which is vastly superior to the mundane, is love. You are a *soul* first. Your natural behavior is how your soul wishes to express itself, but the habits of mortality have imprisoned you. We have addressed how non-attentiveness to the mind has made you an automaton in many ways, and the same goes for when you express yourself intimately.

During intimate communication the focus needs to stay in the heart, not the mind or genitalia. We are used to crude vernacular. We are used to crude humor, and we are used to crude behavior. It is enjoyable to live on a higher plane. You are not your nerve endings—**you are a soul. You cannot feel love through your genitalia.** Don't laugh! This is the insanity that plagues us today. People generally think if they perform well sexually they will be loved and appreciated. They make this mistake because of the misleading marketing that pervades our society. There is no performance grading between a husband and wife who are sharing their love physically. Can you see how perverted the very notion is? **Think of making love as a time for spiritually communicating your love to your spouse.** The physical pleasure will be much greater even though your focus is completely off the physical. But that is merely a side benefit. The greater pleasure is in the heart. Many say they feel like they lose their minds to the love they feel. Everyone says it is the best experience they ever had.

Nerve endings go numb. Nerve endings have no innate intelligence or awareness. Nerve endings become frayed. Nerve endings dry up. Nerve endings send impulses to the mind, which sorts out all the impulses into pain, pleasure, etc. The mind decides if something is new or boring. The shallowness of the sex act

> **You are a soul —not a bundle of nerve endings. Experience love that is not bound to the flesh.**

when performed in all ways to satisfy the lower mind's desire du jour wears thin quickly. It's always only a matter of time. All that eventually happens is individuals become freaked out because *making love* just ain't what it used to be. Yes it is! It just became boring or worse. It's limited when it's physical. Physical is by nature limited. The common (as in lowbrow) wisdom is wrong. Sex toys and lingerie won't help your love grow. It will merely put off the boredom and depression that comes from serving the physical body... get it? I don't want to belabor the point, but I want you to understand it well. You cannot experience infinite love through finite means.

The human soul wants to express love even through the vehicle of the body. The way to do this is by raising the energy that is stuck in the area of the genitals and move it up to the heart. Or, as the case may be, move the energy down from the mind to the heart. This manipulation of energy is done through the use of will power and imagination. Open the door in your heart and allow the liquid love to flow out and in...while making love...wait! Do you understand the principles here? You are consciousness, which is essentially energy. You, as love, can flow toward and into and around your spouse. You can engulf each other with ever-growing, uncontained love. When you want to move your arm or leg, you *will* it to happen. You move the energy to your muscles, which then do the mechanical work. In the case of moving the subtle energy of love, the same process takes place. First, you decide to do it—volition. Then, you use your imagination to visualize it happening. Lastly, you move it.

Do not come to each other with your horniness, which is *completely* physically driven. Go to each other with your hearts. In your unseen heart is the reservoir of love. That is why you can actually *feel* love in your heart. Visualize your heart opening or your heart melting or whatever works for you. Visualize it in your heart, not in your mind. Activate the flow of your love and ignore all other mental and bodily signals. The more you practice this the more you will enjoy it. It is the habituated mind with its doubts and fears that may make this exercise seem difficult, but it is *your* mind and you can make it happen if you choose. Push away all doubts. Focus as best you can and deny any discouraging toughts. The proof of this method is in the doing.

Do not come to each other with your horniness, which is completely physically driven. Go to each other with your hearts.

From now on, have a different purpose for your intimate encounters. All your past notions should be put aside so that you can experience what is meant to be experienced. Instead of having sex, you will go to your marriage partner with the intention of exchanging love vows in the form of energy. **This is not some lofty philosophy. This is the real deal!** You will be metaphorically switching your attention from the foam washing up on the shore to the ocean and waves and sunset and view of the mountains—and you will still have the foam washing up on the shore. The act of making love will take on the higher purposes divulged here and experienced at many different levels. No boredom! No need to experiment with toys or swinging or porno, etc. You will have an infinite playground to play in and as long as you put your love into the space, you will have one memorable experience after another.

The man's purpose for intimacy is to demonstrate appreciation and protection, as well as express humble love. This is the time to adore your wife.

The woman's purpose for intimacy is to demonstrate loyalty and appreciation, as well as express humble love. This is the time to adore your husband.

Husband: No longer see your wife as a means of relieving the sexual pressure. It is a demeaning thought. It's not her job to relieve you. In the beginning, as you develop your new thought habits it is a good idea to masturbate some hours before your time together so you can go to your precious wife undistracted by the animal kicking you and beating you up.

Wife: In the beginning your husband will be struggling within as he subdues the beast. His body will be torturing him. Be patient and understanding without judgment. You likely need to connect with him by relieving him in the early encounters (as your expression of love) while he learns to experience the security of love without an orgasm (an orgasm is not taboo, its fine, but the focus must change). It may take some time. Some husbands will never quite get there all the way. But showing unconditional love will be his greatest incentive. This area is the domain of the heart, and you are far more natural in it. *Teach* only by example. He will discover the superiority of love over sex while making love through experience and without pressure. Never punish him by thinking less of him or expressing expectations. Know that he is being punished enough through his attachment to the brutality of physical attachment.

From now on, you will have a different purpose for your intimate encounters

Now that you understand the science in theory the following structured experiment will provide the proof

Plan your encounters as spiritual events. You will exchange love in a temple. Your bedroom is your sanctuary. Make sure you dedicate your time to being with each other one hundred percent. Be excited and enthusiastic. Look forward to the experience as if it is your first and possibly last chance to show your love and respect.

Follow these important steps in the beginning:

- Be clean (bathe and trim and apply deodorant/perfume).

- Be very courteous.

- Be very sweet.

- Be complimentary.

- Be grateful.

- Prepare the room to be romantic with soft light and, if you like, candles, incense, soft music, or whatever relaxes you.

- No alcohol! Learn to be comfortable by looking into each other's eyes and lightly touching.

- Wear one layer of loose clothing —perfume if you wish.

- Make no fast movements.

- Look into each other's eyes and communicate with words such as "You look beautiful and I love you. May I kiss you?"

- Keep your eyes open.

- Open your hearts and pour love from your heart.

- Open your heart and feel the love pouring in/out.

- Keep your energy, your attention, at the heart.

- Take turns, only a couple of minutes each, touching each other's hair, shoulders, etc.

- Appreciate each other, look at each other, compliment each other, and adore one another.

- Connect genitally very slowly and deliberately—no blind

thrusting. Use your hands gently, very gently. This connection should not happen for <u>at least</u> twenty or thirty minutes.

- The first touch of the genitalia does not mean now its time for intercourse. The goal is intimacy, not immediate penetration.

- Gently hug and release each other.

- This is not hump day. Those days must go. This is an expression of love and must transcend lust.

- It may be that you have no intercourse, but ladies take note! If your man has been stimulated and you don't help him get relief, it is like dangling ice cream in front of your kids all day and then telling them they are greedy for wanting some.

- Out of love and compassion, without judgment and with joy, you need to help your husband ejaculate. He will eventually, maybe, rise above that. But that's his business and not what I advocate.

- Once connected, move only very slowly or not at all; feel the heart.

- Don't think or worry about wet or dry, soft or hard; focus on the heart.

- If you have orgasms, push the energy up to the heart; focus on the heart.

- Hold each other; focus on the heart.

- Relax in the arms of your true love.

- Feel loved and eternally connected.

Going about your expressions of intimacy in this way will be very fulfilling and memorable. It does not preclude some sexual exhilaration or the intimacy of oral sex, but the focus will be on love—on the sweet love in your united hearts surrounding you. Use this format exclusively for at least three months. Your bedroom is yours, and you can do what you wish. The point is that if you go with lust often enough it will drown you in sensory delusion.

Finale

I have done my best to share this vital information with you.

I pray with all my heart it is useful to you for the good of your family.

The nutshell version of this whole thing is pretty simple:

1. Treat your spouse with incredible love and kindness.

2. Be grateful for the little things you receive.

3. Never, ever blame or criticize.

God blesses you.

CPSIA information can be obtained
at www.ICGtesting.com
Printed in the USA
BVHW011711011219
565294BV00004B/158/P

9 780578 017495